Zona:
Her Collected Works
and then some

Zona: Her Collected Works
and then some

Poetry and Prose of a Mother
Memories of Her Son & His Son

Zona Gail Chapman Samples

collected and edited by
John Chapman Samples
& **John Wayne Samples**

2Close2TheGround Publishing
Noblesville, Indiana
Printed in the USA

ISBN-10: 0-69249-103-1
ISBN-13: 978-0-69249-103-4

© 1977 & 2015 by John Samples

This book consists of poetry, nonfiction stories, and recollections.
All rights reserved.

Zona: Her Collected Works and then some, 2nd Edition
© 2015 by John Samples and 2Close2TheGround Publishing
Some material previously published under prior copyrights in 1977 and 2013

All rights reserved. Without the expressed permission of the author, no part of this publication may be reproduced, stored in a retrieval system or transmitted in any way by any means, electronic, mechanical, photocopy, recording or otherwise, without including the copyright notice and attribution to the author(s).

Published by
2Close2TheGround Publishing
Noblesville, Indiana 46060-1021

The publisher believes we are all broken pilgrims on a journey in search of God the Father. Our publications feature works of fiction and nonfiction that tell stories of stubbed toes and crashed angels and healing and getting back up.

Cover design and interior layout by JSam Communications • www.JSam.com

---

Published and printed in the United States of America.

ISBN-10: 0-69249-103-1
ISBN-13: 978-0-69249-103-4

Also from 2Close2TheGround

The Father, The Son, & The Brother's Ghost
A Tragedy and a Trilogy

JSamPlays
for Church Groups
and Faith Applications

Available online at Amazon.com, CreateSpace.com, www.JSam.com, and other retail outlets.

Composed by -
- Zona Chapman Samples -

The signature page from Zona's poetry ledger

Table of Contents

Her Beginnings

Her Faith

Her Nature

Her Sundry Thoughts

Her Home & Family

Her Lover

Her Three Sons

Her Grandchildren

...and then some

Her Endings

194 Z.C.S

God's Unwritten Laws

Unwritten laws strengthening
hands
Staying ones feet from
forbidden lands.
They are not written with
an iron pen.
But are stronger than reasoning
in the hearts of men.
God's Chastening rod that
proves his love
and leads our hearts to rest
above.
The musical sound in the
tone of a chord.
praise of a soul pregnant
with the spirit of the Lord.
The whisperings for youth
The memories for age
These things are not written
on any page.
The measureless dimensions
of God's great love.
The length and breadth
and heights above
The wideness of his mercy
The mystery of his grace
The innocence seen in
a child's sweet face.

Z.S

195 Z.C.S.

Quotation

"The mysterious voice speaks
and a gleam of faith
glows through the darkness
Love breathed a prayer
and God was there
comforting manna fell
like gentle rain from
Heaven"

Z.C.S.

please read me the words
From those red letter pages.
Read those comforting words
Its the last for me you can do.
They were spoken by Jesus
My Lord and my Savior
As the Father loved me
So I have loved you"
Read me precious words
From those redletter pages
In the book that is edged in Gold
So dear to my heart
Are the words of my Savior
precious comforting words
They never grow old.

"Come unto me and I will
give you rest."

Z.G.S.

My time and my strength
So soon they are leaving
My suffering here-So soon
will be o'er
Let your hearts rejoice
Loved ones don't be grieving
But meet me in Heaven
To live ever more.

Zona's "poetry ledger"

Forward

by Her Son

Romanticism, melancholia, nobility, and piety may seem strange and out of place in prose and poetry about the hill people of Kentucky, especially to those unlearned in the true ways of mountain folk. Just listen in these pages to the incessant drumbeat of a call to excellence of thought in the writings of Zona Gail (Chapman) Samples.

Born in 1902 in Lee County, she grew up on Bear Creek near Beattyville and Canyon Falls, Kentucky, in the foothills of the Cumberland Mountains. Here she learned of country ways and, thanks to some Missionary school workers, she also heard the luring call of higher thoughts early in life.

My mother met her soulmate in Floyd Byrd Samples (1900–1979) during a convention at the Mt. Zion Christian Church near Millers Creek, Kentucky, and on November 22, 1927 they were married at Beattyville by William Warner. To this marriage God added three sons: Floyd Byrd "Junior" (1929–1991), Walter Roscoe "Buster" (1931–1976), and myself, John "C." Chapman (1933–).

There are echoes in my memory of this simple country girl gathering her three sons about her of the evening and reading aloud from the Holy Bible, and occasionally from the master poets. Her formal education concluded with one year of High School at Berea, Kentucky, but her learning never stopped. In addition to studying nursing before getting married, she worked at reading great writers. Then *she* began to write.

This book reflects only a portion of her works. Some of these are from her 'poetry ledger,' one of Dad's accounting books in which she wrote many of her poems, thoughts, and reminders to her life. A lot of these pieces I have received in letters from her over the years, and several more we have found here–and–there since her death in 1988—from storage lockers to hidden gems tucked inside a Bible or random book.

I know there are many more verses and essays out there, or at least there used to be. For example, friends and family spread around Kentucky and Ohio may still have some cherished favorites that Mom may have shared only with them; perhaps this publication will lead to more 'discoveries' that will result in a future edition revealing additional expressions of this woman's prolific thinking and writing.

Whether it's rhyming verse or purposeful prose, much—and maybe most—of her poetry was created during some sort of common correspondence where she was just sharing her heart or the routine of her day. In my mind, her words would leap off the page with a perhaps unintended rhythm. Extracting those expressions from the lined paper on which they were born in longhand has been a joy renewed. Also, working on this updated edition with my own son has brought new insights and even more delight (or at least that's what he wrote here for me as he edited the manuscript).

If you should recognize some of the lines of Mother's poems as coming from other poet's pens, it is assuredly unintentional. Some of her words feel familiar even after a first reading, and we have made concerted efforts to ensure these are all truly original. There are some obvious uses of existing titles (such as *"Are All the Children In,"* which was also a song popularized by Johnny Cash), but we are content that virtually all—and we believe it to be ALL—of these verses were crafted from Mother's own mind and pen. She read widely and was certainly influenced by the writings of others, from scriptures to the classics; if some phrases of unknown poets have lodged in her mind and endured the purifying filtration of her Godly thinking —then those writers should be complimented.

Our effort to categorize her works has been daunting as nearly every piece has a component of faith, family, and history. We didn't worry too much about chronology because we simply don't know when a lot of these were written. We've included the dates that we know—and some of those do tell a story when connected to life and world events that would be on her mind as she wrote. But then again, it seems as though we were *all* on her mind as she wrote, without regard to time or place.

We can't help but wonder what she would think about her simple words and prayers being shared with you in this way. Our hope is that this will allow her to speak to your soul and to your heart—and even to your smile—the way her voice has stayed fresh with us for so many years.

– John Chapman Samples

Floyd Sr, John C. &
Zona Samples
1978

Note from JW:

My earliest memory of a book—either in my hands or being read to me—is "*The Best Loved Poems of the American People,*" selected by Hazel Felleman and published in 1936 by Garden City Publishing. This treasure of verse was in Granny's library and I cannot remember a visit to her home when I did not spend time with this collection, either alone or with her reading from it. A warn copy still sits in a prominent place in my home among my other favorite reads. This was my introduction to written imagery. Granny was my introduction to written emotions.

Dedication

by Her Son's Son

Like her first book of published poetry (printed 'privately' in 1977 on the occasion of their 50th wedding anniversary), this edition is dedicated to my grandmother, Zona Samples, and her steadfast husband of more than five decades, my grandfather, Floyd Samples, Sr.

Almost every page in this book reveals some part of their life together and how their partnership was marked by integrity, trust, faithfulness, godliness and joy. Their marriage had financial setbacks and its share of tragedies, but through it all the vows they took so seriously were held sacred and inviolate. Through it all there was love. Through it all there was music. Through it all there was much laughter, often around a good card game of Rook (Kentucky rules).

After years of that first hardcover publication being used as a reference for sermon illustrations and personal refreshment, it is time to re-fresh and update her collected works, and for the first time ever make Granny's pen and down-home philosophies available to the whole world through this paperback edition.

This book also honors the years of ministry by her son—my father—John C. Samples, and his thousands of sermons that often included quotes from these verses. The youngest of Zona and Floyd's three sons, Dad turned 82 as we were working on this project together.

– John Wayne Samples

Dr. Vince Alig
1927–2015

Acknowledgment

Dr. Vincent Alig of Indianapolis was a great encourager to both of us. He challenged us when we taught and applauded us when we fought through the shallows to get to the depths of scripture.

It was his appreciation and affection for many of the poems written by Mom/Granny that led to our decision to tackle the project that has become this book, particularly when he specifically insisted that this was something we *needed* to do—if not for her, then for the rest of us.

Dr. Alig passed away just a few days before the first-draft printing of *Zona: Her Collected Works and then some.*

That saddened us at first, but then we realized he can now hear these verses directly from the author.

Thank you for finishing well, Vince, and for pushing us to finish this.

–The Samples Boys

Her Beginnings

Zona Gail Chapman in her early 20s, circa 1925

Sounds of Eternity

When I am no more visible
And the touch of life is gone.
Here in these pages you will find me
Where I've spent many hours alone.
Alone from the world's mad rushing;
Alone from the sight of things.
Not really alone, only hushing
To listen to the inner voice sing.
It is singing always in the spirit,
In the life in the soul of me,
And the sound I hear is immortal
Sweet strains of eternity.

Golden Years

My ambition is
and always has been
to be worthy of respect,
to live and walk in the Spirit of a Christian
until it becomes more natural to do the right
as it does to do other things that aren't right.
I know I haven't reached perfection,
but are we not what we think we are
after all?

Dad and I
are living in the golden years;
the finishing years of a long Journey,
I think.
You can compare us to children
anxious to get to our new home,
curious but with unfaltering steps,
ready for the evening sunset
in the golden west.
Waiting to cross the silent river,
looking for the luminous footprints
of the Master
which only the blessed can see.

All life's discords we have woven into harmony;
hand in hand we count the golden stars.

It's evening time.

Written in the mid-1970s

Floyd & Zona on their wedding day, November 22, 1927

Her Faith

Faith

There are no footprints on the water
Where the blessed master walked.
There is no writing
in the restless shifting sands.
But I hear the rustle of his garment
as He talked.
And I touched His precious robe
with my hands.
I walked into the waters
of the Red Sea place of life
with a faith that's hard to understand.
I heard Him say "Be not afraid,
No harm can come to Thee
though ten thousand fall
at thy right hand."

Faith Is

Faith is the substance of things we do not see.
It is the melodious sound of a Heaven's eternity.
Faith tastes the fruit while the seed are beneath the sod,
and offers loving Grace to an ever-living God.
Faith is a mother's love as she prays for a wayward child
and sees the man of her hopes on whom the Lord will smile.
Faith looks through darkest clouds where storms and tempests
are in darkest hours and sees a bright and shining star.
Faith is the wayfarers map as he journeys the Jericho road
and sees through the chariots' dust,
rest, in the city of God.

Faith is the minister's oath
as he tears the barriers down
in his compassion for lost souls,
though he wears the martyr's crown.
Faith is the book of life,
and its shining record tells
that it's serenely kept in a Christian heart
to a God who makes all things well.

He is the Way

I stood behind the crowd and heard their cries
so long—so loud.
I saw his blood-drops cleanse them
of their sin.
I begged to find my way within.

I groped along;
it seemed so hard
To find a place
that's near the Lord.
I felt alone,
afraid, despised,
And then I saw His loving eyes
So near I couldn't understand.
He stood so still
with out stretched hand.
I offered mine,
my soul was free.
My Savior's blood had then touched me.
Oh cleansing blood, oh love divine.
All glory to that friend of mine.
I love Him better every day
Since I found him,
He is the way.

Look to Jesus

If you are lost
    Look for his footprints.
If you are cold
    His robe you may wear.
If you are hungry,
    sit, he will feed you.
The bread of life He will always share.

Don't be discouraged
    Keep in touch with the Master;
If you are tired
    He will give you rest.
In life's darkest hours
    A light he offers.
If you are weary
    Lean on His breast.

I Thank Thee Lord

I thank Thee Lord
For happy years.
For comfort when
You saw my tears.
For health and strength
To do Thy will.
And my small place
On earth to fill.
For chastening Lord,
That proved your love;
Your promise of
Sweet rest above.
When all my earthly
Tasks are done,
And my soul's battles
Have been won;
I Thank Thee Lord.

How to Walk with Christ

Must I visit Canaan's land
Or walk by Galilee's sea
To feel the touch of the Master's hand
Or place my feet where he used to be?
Must I conquer the mighty storm
Or still the raging sea
Before I feel His strengthening arm
Or His mercy held out to me?
Wherever I find a human heart,
All burdened down with care,
And help him make another start,
Won't I find Christ's footprints there?

World

Just one world—among a million
One lost sheep—among the spheres
This old world is but an atom;
God's footstool through endless years.

From God's mercy seat in heaven
He beholds this fallen world.
Are his other worlds all sinless
With His Holy flag unfurled?

He sent His son for just one purpose,
To redeem this world from sin.
Silence there will be in Heaven
When our Lord returns again.

March 13, 1964

Ruth

Ask me not to leave thee, Oh kiss me not good-bye;
Please mother take me with you, there I'll remain until I die.
Your people I will love them. Your God is my God too.
Oh please do not forsake me. I want to go with you.

Naomi

Your sister, do you see her? She beckons you to come.
Go back unto your people. My child, stay with your home.

Ruth

Where'er you go I am going. Where you stay I will stay.
You're the only one who loves me
since God took my husband away.

Naomi

Weep not my child but follow, my God shall be yours too.
My people, they will love you. Go bid your sister adieu.
I love you precious daughter, you are sweeter than seven sons,
And God will bless you greatly; through you his Son is born.

TV / Tender Vespers

In the early days of my life, I can recall the magic of our weekly prayer meetings in our homes. It must have been something like when the early Christians went from house to house.

The atmosphere seemed so sacred, many prayers, many tears of rejoicing, singing songs of praise, reading God's Holy Word discussing the reading of Scriptures. Hard-working people spending their vesper hour once a week, to come together in humbleness and love to God and for each other. Teaching Jesus to the children and living so as to be an example to them.

Would to God we could have hours like those now instead of sitting in front of a TV set bored to tears by that silliness of foolish pictures. Children seeing shooting and killing and sex and hearing profanity instead of prayer.

How long is God going to show mercy to a nation of people who have forgotten him?

I am the Light of the World

I searched for my soul in the darkness,
 I wept from fear of the night.
I heard a voice so gentle
 Which said, "I am the light."
I lost my way in the dessert
 Amid much fear and strife,
So soft like the voice of an angel
 One said, "I am the life."
While wandering in lanes of anguish
 'midst ruins of death and decay
A whisper amid the tumult;
 "I am the way."
A voice that's quieter than silence
 We may hear in the days of our youth,
Whispering to all who will listen,
 "I am the truth!"

Silent Night

There was no pillow for His head.
There was no cover for His bed.
But there was moonlight's golden gleam,
And a young mother's heavenly dream.
The night was silent. A Holy Night.
Though to the shepherds all was bright.
For they had heard the angels sing
And came to see the new born King.
Today I walked to Bethlehem
Nor did I walk alone.
The Christ child of the manger
Came down from Heaven's throne.
And walked with me to his home town,
And the glory shown the world around.
For where we walked was Holy Ground.

December 19, 1971

Now!

For when God's patience turns to wrath,
and one walks forbidden paths,
and waits too long,

Woe to those who are at ease
in worldly pleasure
doing as they please,

Then chance is gone.
One is left in bleak despair.
No time to repent, no use for prayer.

A hardened heart, sharp stabbing pains
of sad regret,
when on one's soul the sun has set,
And God departs.
Now is the accepted time.

Tomorrow never comes.

The Weavers

We weave our dreams
        on the loom of life,
Weaving each thread with care.
        The colors of red and blue and white
Each color mingled with prayer.

We think of red as our Saviors blood,
        The blue, the kingdom of heaven.
The white means purity of souls
        For whom God's son was given.
The Lord of love inspects our dreams
        As we work at our tiresome task
And we raise our thirsty souls
        To His touch.
And with trembling lips we ask,
        Lord we are tired,
        we have worked at the weaving,
        Until we are weak and old.
Lend us of your thread and relieve our grieving;
        And the thread He gave was gold.
Golden dreams of heavens fair city
        Interwoven in the fruit of our loom.
Beautiful dreams and they bring sweet courage
        To the weary and toil worn.

The Sea

And I saw a new heaven and a new earth;
For the first heaven and the first earth
were passed away and the sea is no more.

The sea separates land from land—
    people from people.
Among God's people there is a sea of
    misunderstanding, of enmity, of jealousy,
    of suspicion, of death.
But in heaven there will be nothing
    to separate brother from brother.
Spiritual ties will be
    unbroken.
For God's people will be
    united in eternity.
In that wonderful world where the wicked
    cease from troubling,
    and the weary are at rest.
No more sea of separation—
    No more sea of pain—
        No more sea of unrest—
            No more sea of pain or death.

Prepare Us for the Conflict

Prepare us for the conflict
        Equipped as men of war.
With armor buckled on afresh
        Our spirits swords of fire.
Under the leadership of a captain,
        Who never lost a fight.
May we hold aloft the banner
        That stands for God and right.
And when the race is over,
        and the battles have been won.
May we hear the cry of victory,
        Hear the Captain say, "well done.
Lay aside your armor,
        Hang your sword on Jasper walls.
Enter into grandeur
        where shadows never fall."

1973

Man

When man thinks of his apparent littleness
seemingly he is but a grain of sand on a
dessert—a drop of water in an ocean—
when he compares his physical being
with the universe in which he lives,
Why should God think of him
or visit him with such marvelous mercy?
Yet a man was created in the image of God,
        a little lower than the angels.
He was given dominion
        over all creation.
God's greatest work is not a planet,
a shining sun or a celestial city of singing angels,
        But Man.
If in times to come that we must
stand condemned in the presence of God
and Christ, it will not be because they
have failed to love us, but simply because
we have refused to abide in their love.
We can't afford to fail.
        Read God's Word.
        Obey His will.

January 19, 1975

Anchored

I could not sleep
Were not my soul
Anchored in Thee.
Oh, God, I could not be stedfast
Were not my soul
Anchored in Thee.
I could not be sure
I could not bear my cross
Were not my faith
Anchored in Thee.
I could not bear the darkness
Without your presence in my soul.
I thank Thee God
For your son Jesus
Who made it possible
For me to sleep
To be stedfast
To be sure
To bear my cross
Thank you for grace
To anchor my soul
in peace with Thee.

Just a Garden of Prayer

When my candle of faith
        Flickers dangerously low
And in prayer I kneel
        And to his mercy seat go,
The clamor of doubt
        and confusion will cease;
Into my spirit flows
        great inner peace.
My world may be small,
        Just a garden of prayer
But all of God's great loving
        mercy is there.
The path is illumined
        By his kindness revealed.
His great loving spirit,
        My sword and my shield.

Wait With Patience

There are those whom we love
And we pray for,
Yet they spurn all our anxious fears.
But we know not the path the soul travels
And we wait with patience the years.

Yet we have a true faith to lean on;
We're strong through the strength, of our Lord.
And the vision will change in due season,
While we trustfully live by His word.

So we lose the world and its troubles
After we have done our all.
Leave the rest to the Lord of the Heavens,
For He promised to answer our call.

A Mother's Prayer for her Minister Son

Just a word of love repeating
In this morning's early greeting.
This to let you know I care
And include you in my prayer.

It's so cheerful to have a feeling
That the spirit is revealing.
You're so much of my life, a part,
You are the joy of my heart.
And I hope that you are drinking
From the fountain of my thinking.
And the spirit fills you there,
As it fills your mother here.

God's love is without human measure
And he trusts us with his treasure.
And when we minister to men,
His holy presence, we feel within.

Fairfax Beginning

For when God's patience turns to wrath
And one walks forbidden paths,
        And waits too long,
Woe to those who are at ease
In worldly pleasure doing as they please.
        Then chance is gone.
One is left in bleak despair.
No time to repent, No use for prayer.
        A hardened heart.
Sharp stabbing pains of sad regret
When on one's soul the sun has set,
        And God departs.

Now is the accepted time,
Tomorrow never comes. . .

Written in the fall of 1968 on the occasion of John C. Samples assuming the pulpit at Fairfax Christian Church in Indianapolis, Indiana

Fairfax Christian Church, Indianapolis, Indiana

Prayer for a Deep Water Fairfax Fisherman

Blessed is the man that walketh
    not in the counsel of the ungodly,
    nor standeth in the way of sinners,
    nor sitteth in the seat of the scornful,
But his delight is in the law of the Lord and in his law doth he meditate day and night.

Yes, I think my little boy has really gone fishing in deep water —you have really cast your net on the other side—but don't doubt, and don't worry; use tact and trust God.

You are not the little shepherd boy playing on the harp now
    you will fight with the beasts at Ephesus
    you may bait with Samples of love
But you'll need to use the sword of the Spirit.

Let no wave of tale bearing or gossip influence; just preach the Gospel loud and clear. Sects, clans, and enemies from without and within will vanish without harm to you when chased by the Holy Spirit.
You are not to judge,
    that isn't your mission,
    but be right and be positive.

Don't even start catering to people—you can't in a large place like that—they would do you to death.

You can be firm and you'll have to.
I know you can.
Your heart is tender
but it's also strong
and true for Christ's sake.

I know you will grow stronger by having strenuous work to do. But God makes no mistakes and I believe He has placed you there because He has a work for you to do.

So no matter how hard—do it well with his help
and Mother will follow you in prayers
every step of the way.

Worshiping Together, Apart

Dear Son,

Please let me be in church with you this morning.

I didn't go to Church here, you see; my aches and pains increase daily and I don't want to bore people by talking about them, so I'll not go into details. Just say, "Welcome, Mother."

> Let me walk down the aisle and see your heartfelt smile, words spoken with love inspired and I'll feel the presence of the glorified Lord.
>
> I shall eat for my soul is hungry.
> I shall drink to quench my spiritual thirst.
> I'll enjoy the congregation with wonderful sweet accord, for I know the fine people in your church group are people who love the Lord.

Well thanks, it's been wonderful worshiping with thee.
I just wonder if somewhere in your thoughts,
you really thought of me.

My prayers in your sermon always,
–Mother

November 6, 1966

What will the Harvest Be?

What has happened to our world?
    Have the stars gone down and
    left the moonless night in total darkness?
This sound of hoof beats on the
Hardened brains of men.
Have Satan's workers of evil
Been paroled for a season
To plant the seed of lust
For blood and greed, for
power in men's hearts?
Oh, what will the harvest be?

Note:

In 1971 I began working with a new congregation in West Lafayette, Indiana. We did not have our own church building and we were invited by the Rabbi of Temple Israel to use their building, "...since they weren't using it on Sundays."

Rabbi Levinson and I became good friends through the years we were there. During one of our many conversations I mentioned that a book from my mother's library that had helped me during my ministry studies was a work on human nature entitled "Peace of Mind" by Rabbi Joshua Liebman. He smiled and shared with me that Rabbi Liebman had once served the same congregation that was now hosting us at Temple Israel—one of the oldest Jewish congregations in Indiana.

– John C.

TO: West Lafayette Christian Church

Today I went where men of God
adore Thee,
And uncovered their hearts
before Thee.
The harmony of the hour
that teaches Christian power.
When before Thy throne hearts kneel,
Sacred fellowship reveals,
God was there—
There were no strangers there today
And to my mind the thought was given;
The friendliness of people here
Is close akin to Heaven.

May 23, 1976
After visiting the church meeting in Temple Israel
West Lafayette, Indiana

Red Letter Pages

My time and my strength
So soon they are leaving
My sufferings here soon will be o'er.
Let your hearts rejoice.
Loved ones don't be grieving
But meet me in heaven
To live evermore.
Please read me the words
From these red letter pages.
From that book that is edged in gold.
So dear to my heart are the words of my Savior,
Precious words that will never grow old.
Read again the sweet words
From those red letter pages.
Read those comforting words
It's the most you can do.
Words spoken by Jesus,
My Lord and my Savior.
"As the Father loved me
So I have loved you."
Listen to His loving words,
"Come unto me, weary one come home,
There is sweet rest for thee."

I Heard His Voice

I heard his voice
In the new born baby's cry,
In the sigh of the saint
When he came to die.
I heard His voice
In the morning fair,
Again with my burden
He helped me bear.
I heard His voice
In the sadness of night
When a sinner turned
And sought the light.
I heard His voice
When hope seemed gone,
When I stood on the brink
Hopeless and alone.
I heard His voice
And courage came,
With hope and with love
His spirit remained.

January 1, 1969

Empty Shell

Like an empty shell that lies alone
I'll be here no more—the pearl is gone.
Springtime will fade, and summer come,
But a voice you loved will then be dumb.

The melancholy night winds drear
Remind you I'm no longer here.
But—all is well, don't weep for me,
For with my Savior I will be.
Awaiting in that heaven fair,
For the ones I've loved to enter there.

Would I Could

Would I could have been with the Father
When the world was still and quiet.
Would I could have heard his voice
When he said "Let there be light!"
Would I could have known his Eden
And with him lingered there.
Would I could have seen his sunrise
On that sinless morn so fair.
Would I could have seen the mist rise
Above the watered flowers.
Attended the first marriage
And witnessed that holy sinless hour.

Assurance

When I stay close to Him my skies are blue,
My heart sings praise, and friends are true.
I drink from clear waters that issue from the rock.
I distribute food to the hungry, bring joy to the flock.
When I walk with Him—My Savior and My Lord—
The high hills are a refuge, there is peace in His word.
He walks on the waters, yes, on the wings of the wind.
His chariot rideth the clouds, yet He is my friend.
When others forget me, He is ever near.
When hours are the darkest He frees me from fear.
So I will walk with Him until I am called away
And angels bear my soul to a land of endless day.

December 28, 1976

Lest I Myself Should be a Castaway

Thy confidence I pray dear Lord,
As I walk on stepping stones.
When on your errands I must go,
Don't let me walk alone.
Sometimes it's difficult to see,
The margin seems so small,
And lest my foot should miss a step,
oh, Lord don't let me fall.
Let me drink alone at Thy table Lord,
Nor dare to take one sup.
Protect me from temptation Lord,
To drink of the devil's cup.
And though it be my lot dear God
To walk where martyrs trod,
May I pick up the bloody cross
And follow them dear God.

May 17th, 1972

Always Building

You are building a church.
The ground has been cleared,
You've accepted his person
And believed in His word.
The foundation is rock
And the structure is gold,
The interior is love.
It's the home of your soul.
It is garnished with jewels,
Kind deeds you have done,
For the glory of God
And belief in His son.
You are measuring daily
To God's holy plan,
The saving of sinners
The serving of man.
You have opened a fountain,
Pure waters so clear,
And invited the thirsty
His message to hear.
Oh come to the fountain;
It's waters are free,
Accept God's salvation,
'twas purchased for thee.

My Candle

When my candles of faith flicker dangerously low
And in prayer I kneel and to His mercy seat go,
The clamor of doubt and confusion will cease
And into my spirit flows great inward peace.
My world may be small—just a garden of prayer,
But all of God's great loving mercy is there.
The path is illumined by His kindness revealed
His great loving spirit, My sword and my shield.

What to Do??

He is a sinner? Who am I?
Once a sinner too.
If I plead with him
And he scoffs at me
Didn't I do that too?
If he is lost because I failed.
What am I going to do??

"God may have a million worlds
We only have one."

Enchanted Path

Where will I find the Christ Child?

He will hear me when I pray.

In the preaching of His Gospel

He lived in your church one day.

One day in the morning service

In souls was love divine,

When you brought Christ's Gospel message,

Little minister of His and mine.

He walks among your members,

The spiritual in one accord,

Yes, the enchanted path to your church

Leads one to Christ the Lord.

Christmas 1976

Watchman, What of the Night?

I heard the midnight cry,
The Lord passed over a smitten land,
The first born had to die.
Watchman what of the night?
I heard the tempests roar
In the pearly mists of morning,
Is the blood upon the door?
Watchman, what of the night?
The morning doeth appear,
The Lord said "Take your families
and tarry no longer here."
But Watchman what of the night?
In this war torn modern world,
Is the blood upon the door?
Has God's banner been unfurled?
Watchman, what of the night?
Are they ready for the morn?
They drink from golden vessels
and their revelry goes on.

March 10, 1968

Vision

It is sweet to be in your presence Lord.
Please may my prayers ascend
Here in the quietness of my study Lord,
At the long day's end.
Make me a chart for tomorrow Lord,
Take the day in your control.
Give me vision and courage Lord.
Help me Lord to make your goal.

There are paths for me untrodden Lord,
There are heights yet unattained.
When my heart is bruised and broken Lord,
Please dear Lord relieve the pain.
The battle of life is raging Lord,
May I never know retreat.
Your word shall be my weapon Lord,
And a lantern for my feet.

Mary, the Mother of Jesus; Her News

Mary was engaged to Joseph, a man of God's royal family.
To Mary appeared an Angel.
Mary was highly favored and blessed among women.

"Thou shalt bring forth a son and shall call his name Jesus, and he shall inherit the throne of His father David."

The Holy Ghost came upon her,
the power of the highest o'er shadowed her.
Mary was happy to be so highly favored as to
Be the mother of the Son of God.
Yet Mary loved Joseph and he loved her.
At first he couldn't understand
and he thought on these things
But Mary knew she was innocent and
she was sustained by this knowledge.
Joseph sought to put her away;

Quietly, tenderly he didn't want to hurt the girl he loved —then the angel appeared, And Joseph must have called to memory Isaiah 7:14:

"Behold a virgin shall be with child and shall bring forth a son, and they shall call His name Emmanuel— which being interpreted is, God with us."

Mary, the Mother of Jesus; Her Blooms

For a beautiful portrait of mother
Let us look in the album of God's Word
at Mary the mother of our Lord.
The artist mixed his colors for this portrait
as though he were going to paint
not one but many blossoms
of a delicate and flower-like purity.
She is the modest violet.
Pink for pure love.
The red rose representing
the innocent blood that
must be shed by her Son.
She knew the day would come
when he would travel the lonely
agonizing road to the Cross and
no longer be her baby to
hold in her arms,
to fondle him upon her bosom.
As Mary, all mothers must
follow their sons to the Cross;
God help us if we failed to
guide them right.

Mary, the Mother of Jesus: Her Sermon

Mary was a woman of a good character.
Her habits and her conduct followed
the highest standards, and
God chose her to be the
mother of His Son.

Mary was the vital force of purity.
She will be so honored
all generations shall call her blessed.
The tender impressions of her sweetness
sinks deep in our souls
for she was human
just as you or I.

Her sermon to all mankind
was these words:

"Whatsoever he saith unto you do it."
John 2:5

The Voice of the Master

No one can still the voice of the Master,
He longs in your heart to reign.
Listen, you'll hear for he seeks to enter,
He knocks, and He knocks again.

Come unto me all ye that are weary,
Pass not your life here in vain.
I will give you rest, if you'll only trust me
He knocks, and He knocks again.

What would you do if God should call you
And you refused to attain.
The sinless life He offers to you
If – He – never – knocked – again?

Thoughts

For some small task
O' Lord I ask
Give me an humble duty.
May in life's dark night
I place a light
In your great world of beauty.
"Fear not my child."
It seemed he smiled.
Your timid tongue may falter
But in your simple childish way
You've placed great offerings
On my altar.

"The thoughts within make the world without."

God's Book

When your body and soul
is plunged into sorrow,
And your life seems as dark as night,
There's a lamp in the temple.
There are stars in God's heaven,
Weary pilgrim, look for the light.
Pick up the book lying
there on your table,
the one you've forgotten to read.
It will give you grace, and
will answer your problem,
supply your dark hour's need.
You know this vain world has
nothing to offer
but vanity trouble and care.
Just open God's book,
it's the key to heaven,
And happiness awaits you there.

May 4, 1970

The Hour of Decision

Hallowed is the birthplace of the soul
Where all doubt is conquered,
Where His blood doth make one whole.
Human fear transformed to heavenly faith,
Where one wants the Savior more than life itself;
Lips purified by confession;
A heart cleansed in His blood;
A name recorded in the Book of Life;
A conscience clear and good;
Partaking of communion—mysteries divine;
The holy bond of brotherhood;
Remembering Christ is thine.
The hour of decision;
Place of holy birth;
Relieved of sins great burden;
The sweet peace on earth.

I Shall Help the Helper

Heavenly Father, Give me vision
    And a lantern I may hold.
I, in some way, to help my brother
    As he struggles brave and bold.
I would not sit by in leisure
    While great burdens he must bear.
Though I cannot feed the hungry
    My small basket I may share.
With your blessings Holy Father
    He the multitude can feed,
Many hearts for you are hungry
    Give Him grace to fill their need.
No I cannot bring the message
    Of your holy words divine.
I'll go with him to the wedding
    Where the water's turned to wine.
When the powers of Satan stab him
    and would his holy work deface.
Let me gently stand beside Him
    To wipe blood stains from His face,
When the hours of time have taken
    My last days away from me,
Keep Him in thy service Father;
    Use him where you'd have him be.

"Put your words in his mouth
and the mouths of his children
And their children henceforth
and forever." (Isaiah 59:21)

My Mansion

I live in a mansion that was built for me.
I live in a building the world cannot see.
My heart has its treasures far better than gold.
My mind has a vision that's grand to behold.
I travel to Egypt—then come back again.
I stop in a city called Jerusalem.
I see Him on a mountain and I hear His prayer, too,
"Father, forgive them; they know not what they do."
Hope is an anchor steadfast and sure.
A glimpse of His glory strength to endure.
When troubles assail me and I long for sweet rest,
I find sweet seclusion on the dear Savior's breast.
It's my haven of refuge when troubles are sore.
Clashing storms cannot harm me,
I'm safe evermore.

I live in a mansion that was built for me
When he paid all my debts on Calvary's tree.
I thank you for leaving your footprints so plain;
I travel to Bethlehem and I see the young King.
I hear angels' voices; as a message they sing.
John calls in the wilderness; his message is grand:
Repent for the Kingdom of heaven is at hand!

I look in sweet rapture to heaven above,

I see the spirit descend in the form of a dove,

I hear a voice from heaven saying, "this is my Son."

I live in a mansion
That he built for me

I thank you for leaving
your foot prints so plain
I travel to Bethlahem
and I see the young King
I hear angels voices
as a message they sing
John calls in the wilderness
his message is grand
Repent for the kingdom
of heaven is at hand
I looks in sweet Rapture
to heaven above
I see the spirit descend
in the form of a dove
~~like a dove~~
I hear a voice from heaven
saying "This is my son"

An early handwritten version of
My Mansion

I live in a mansion
that he built for me.
I live in a building
the world can-not see
my heart has treasures
far better than gold
my mind has a vision
that is grand to behold.
I travel to egypt
then come back again
I stop in a city
called jerusalem
I see him on a mountain
and I hear his prayer too
Father forgive them
They know not what they do.
Hope has an anchor
steadfast and sure
a glimpse of his glory
and strength to endure
~~I visit a mother in old~~ Bethlahem town
~~with a babe~~ on her bosom
~~and~~
When troubles assail me
my heart cries for rest
I find sweet seclusion
on my Saviors breast
It is my place of refuge
when troubles are sore
clashing storms cannot harm me
I'm safe ever - more.

Heaven

We live but once
Life has no boomerang.
Youth, strength, nor wisdom
Cannot time retain.
Blasts atomic shake the skies,
Unknown planets crash,
The cosmic rays of meteorites
With constellations crash.
So late the hour–
So little time.
The world grows old
But heaven is in its prime.

I searched the world for heaven,
I found not a glimpse of its blue.
I wept for my heart was breaking.
Seemed a veil had hidden my view.
But I found what I sought With the Holy
And the hush of my fretting was gone.
I had found the divine I was seeking
And I heard His voice saying
"Well done."

The Father Watches

His heart has grown old
With its life full of care;
But childlike and gentle,
He sits in his chair
And he gets a great pleasure
From day unto day,
Sitting on his porch
Watching the children play.
Some play the game fair—
Some want to cheat,
They laugh and they cry,
As they play in the street.
What are his thoughts
On the long summer day,
Sitting on his porch
Watching the children play.

There is one who sits on His great white throne,
And watches the children of earth that are grown.
They too play fair, and too, they cheat,
As our Father in heaven watches the street.

God's Unwritten Laws

Unwritten laws; strengthening hands;
Staying one's feet from forbidden lands.
They are not written with an iron pen
But are stronger than reasoning in the hearts of men.
God's chastening rod that proves his love,
And leads our hearts to rest above.
The musical sound in the tone of a chord;
Praises of a soul pregnant with the spirit of the Lord;
The whisperings for youth, the memories for age.
These things are not written on any page.
The measureless dimensions of God's great love;
The length and breadth and heights above;
The wideness of His mercy, the mystery of His grace.
The innocence seen
In a child's sweet face.

Unwritten Laws of God

The measureless dimensions of God's great love,
The length, the breadth, and heights above.
The wideness of His mercy,
The mystery of His grace.
The innocence seen in a child's sweet face,
The musical sound in the tone of a chord,
Praises of a soul, pregnant with the
Spirit of the Lord.
The whisperings for youth and the memories for age,
These things are not written on any page.
God's chastening rod that proves His love
And leads our hearts to rest above.
Unwritten law strengthening hands,
Staying one's feet from forbidden lands.
They are not written with an iron pen
But are stronger than reasoning
In the hearts of men.

I Know a Place

I know a place,
An humble place,
Where blind receive their sight,
And dying captives there are freed
From chains of endless night.

I know a place,
A blessed place,
Where greed and hate shall cease,
And love shall dwell in human hearts,
And all the world find peace.

I know a place,
A sacred place,
Where glorious hope is given,
Where souls ascend the mountain top
And catch a view of heaven.

I know a place,
Of saving Grace,
And Christ the Lord is there.
Where is this haven on earth, you say?
It is the place of prayer.

King Jesus Walked Here

Sometimes when the journey seems hardest
When the sun hides behind the dark cloud,
And life's wine is as bitter as worm-wood,
The voice of the thunder is so loud.
Then I long for the voice of the Master,
My poor lonely heart to cheer.
Then all of a sudden I hear these words,
"King Jesus walked here!"

When I look on the face of a loved one,
That death has taken from me,
I know that God in his wisdom
Knows what is best to be.
Then I search with the light of his promise,
Like the sisters of Lazarus so dear,
And I hear again those comforting words,
"King Jesus too, walked here!"

Helpless and Dependent

I boasted of my health
For great and strong was I.
I accumulated wealth
Prepared to live—not die.
I looked unto myself
The safety road to trod.
But in the tragic moment
I felt my need for God.
My health I lost quite sudden,
My wealth I couldn't keep.
For health and wealth are fleeting things
And I was left to weep.
I'm glad I learned the lesson,
Though I passed under the rod.
Man cannot look unto himself—
He has to lean on God.

June 8, 1970

At the Crossroads

Jesus met me at the crossroads
In the turning point of life—
He was waiting at the junction
Mid all the sin and evil strife.

Only one way straight and narrow,
While the others were so wide,
Then I heard Him whisper softly,
"Fear not, I will be your guide."

Yes, He met me at the crossroads,
Praise His name, I followed Him,
Gave up the world of sinful pleasure,
His guiding light has ne'r grown dim.

He is waiting at the crossroads,
Sinner give your heart to Him.
He'll direct you through the traffic,
Through a world that's full of sins.

December 29, 1975

The Beautiful Gate

He asks for alms
At the beautiful gate,
One who had suffered much.
But the silver and gold
His poor heart received
Had more than the Midas touch.
And people wondered
As he leapt and praised
God's love to his soul revealed,
He had given heed to the call of Christ
And his crippled feet were healed.

Ask not for things
The world may give
But trust and patiently wait.
If you believe
you too will receive
As the lame one at the beautiful gate.

Fair Haven

Don't leave the Fair Haven
When once you have anchored,
Don't launch where there's danger again.
Though south winds blow softly
They're very deceiving
You'll be tossed by the tempest
of darkness and rain.
The stars will be hidden
You'll fall in the quick sands,
Your hope will be taken away,
Don't leave the fair haven
When once you have anchored
Or you'll pray for the coming of day.

The Celestial Vision of my Upper Room

A grateful heart and a bended knee were companions of Paul. He was burdened for his countrymen who were lost in unbelief. But he thanked God for men like Timothy—see him kneel on a dungeon floor, his eyes filled with tears, begging God for strength and wisdom, not for himself but for a young man who stumbles on behind.

"Help him lord; teach him Lord;
fill him Lord keep him humble and ever faithful."

There is no doubt Paul had a great influence on Timothy. It is easy to forecast with certainty, the future of one nurtured by prayer, nourished in faith, converted to Christ, filled with his spirit and exhorted and encouraged by Paul the aged.

Paul speaks humbly. God saved us Timothy. God called us son. Not according to our works—but to his great works have we been honored. He comforted Timothy.

It is through Christ, his blood and his suffering we are saved in this life. But as for you—continue in what you have learned and have firmly believed knowing from whom you learned and how from childhood you have been acquainted with the sacred writings which are able to instruct you for salvation through faith in Jesus Christ.

All scripture is inspired by God and profitable for teaching, for reproof, for correction, and for training in righteousness that the man of God may be complete, equipped for every good work.

II Timothy 3:14–17

I charge thee before God, and the Lord Jesus Christ—
Preach the word; be instant in season, out of season;
reprove; rebuke, exhort with long suffering and doctrine, but watch. I am now ready to depart. The Lord Jesus Christ be with thy spirit.

Celestial Vision of Elisha

In the days of Elisha, the prophet of God, the King of Syria came with his mighty army against the children of Israel. The servant of Elisha said "Alas, my Master! How shall we do?" Elisha replied "Fear not—for they that are with us are more than they that be with them." Elisha prayed and said, "Lord open his eyes that he may see," and the Lord opened the young man's eyes "and behold, the mountain was full of horses and chariots of fire about Elisha." And so it is, the power of God is with those who do His will. He will feed his flock like a shepherd. He will gather the lambs in his arms and carry them in his bosom, gently guiding the young from harm.

Long for Heaven

John 14:1-6

Tonight I long for rest, as never before.

Today I heard a beautiful sermon by Brother Leggett entitled *Ten seconds after death*. All my life I have tried to live as I thought God wanted me to live. The principal thought in my mind—in my life—has been to live for Jesus, to live to please my Master.

Somehow I haven't really given too much thought to receiving the reward; I have always accepted the fact that Heaven is where God has prepared a place for us, and that we do not belong here, and are living for eternity, and it is so...

But tonight I long for that city, that house not made with hands. Heaven is a wonderful place. I couldn't withhold the tears as that little old man described Heaven today. He made it so real —so near—he couldn't have brought to his congregation the vision if he hadn't had Heaven in his soul.

I thank God for great men, great in soul, oh how marvelous, how wonderful, to be able to stand before a thousand people and be conscious of Heaven with all its glory; the light of

Heaven, the love of God radiates in his face until it makes one think of old Stephen.

Yes I long for heaven tonight, I want to go there. I wish my arms were long enough. I wish my soul was big enough, to reach out and take every one with me.

Don't you?

Manna Rain

"The mysterious voice speaks
and a gleam of faith
glows through the darkness
Love breathed a prayer
And God was there
comforting manna fell
like gentle rain from
Heaven"

Z. C. S.

From Zona's ledger:
The mysterious voice speaks...

The Star of Hope

What do you want, oh stainless youth?

"We want to know the fearless truth.

For truth honor and justice we plead,

Then we will be the men the future needs.

Help us to find purpose and plan,

And we pledge to do the best we can.

We shall walk on lonely shores

Where wounded feet have trod.

We are searching for . . .

The star of hope

In the firmament of God."

Preach the Word

He can walk the tranquil waters

He can quiet the stormy sea,

He can give the eyes new vision,

He can make the prisoners free.

He has food to feed the famished,

Turn the water into wine.

He has power to heal diseases;

Wonder-works of the divine.

Tell the story, preach the word,

Christ's living Gospel so good;

Share the blessed son of God,

Christ's universal Brotherhood.

Saturday Night

Dear Ones:

It is Saturday night—Dad and I have been reading and discussing God's Holy Word.

It's times like these that I live for.
Times when someone will talk with me
about God and His goodness.

Our devotion has been based on I Corinthians 13 and the six gifts: prophecy, tongues, knowledge, faith, hope and love. The first three were super-natural, bestowed for the benefit of the infant church. The last three were complete.

They were and are within reach of every Christian. Faith, hope, love.

Faith believes, hope expects, and love—precious love—abides. Faith binds us to God, hope ties us to heaven, love makes us like God and fits us for heaven. They are bread, water and fresh air, of our spiritual existence. God neither believes nor hopes but love is God. It is the fertile soil that gives birth to every virtue known to men on earth or angels in heaven. We are to love God supremely and our neighbor as ourselves. Faith is like Moses standing on Nebo viewing the land of promise, and dying—with a hope as bright as the morning star, yet it fades at the dawning of eternity's day. But love is translated into life and joy, it is immortal. Some of these ideas I read from an article they so fit in our meditation.

Little preacher, we love you. We sat down and listened good at the recording you sent—your own talent, your own personality, speaking the things that become sound doctrine.

The word of God elevates the spirit and it purifies the soul. There is a saying, "Let the preacher preach."

It is your heaven-given duty, carrying God's truths.
Carry on preacher, carry on.

Sometimes I ask God to send me an understanding of His word, hitherto not clear in my mind. Sometimes He answers so plain—through the Spirit and word—that it almost seems super-natural. Praise His holy name.

Earth has no treasures but perish with suing, however precious they be, yet there is a country to which I am going, Heaven holds all to me.

– Mother

April 24, 1971

God's Rose Garden

Lord I bow humbly before your great throne;
Please give me a rose garden I may call my own.
I will attend it with the greatest of care,
No weeds, blight or insects shall ever be there,
I will cultivate my roses
In beauty they shall bloom
Then all the world around
Will enjoy their perfume.

Sometimes a Christian is tried as by fire,
Not always God gives us those things we desire.
I have a rose garden that's mine alone, my son,
With briars and weeds, it's all overgrown.
You are prepared my child,
Will you accept the task?
Go labor in my garden.
Is that too much to ask?

Yes, your hands will be torn by the thorns, that is true,
But you'll have a reward of my blessings on you.
I will bless you greatly for all your toiling hours,
And with dew from heaven I will spray your sweet flowers.
When your work is finished
And from life you depart,
The sweet rose of Sharon
will be blooming in your heart.

Use Me

The world is hungry Lord
Just for Thee
Take me Lord,
Break me Lord
Let me share Calvary.
In this blazing whirl
Of fire and speed.
Cool me Lord
School me Lord
Make me heed.
Take my talent, tune me
For the hour
Lead me Lord
Feed me Lord
And fill my soul with power.
Let not the glitter
Turn my heart from gold
Slow me Lord
Show me Lord
Until thy message is told.

Sometime

Then be content poor heart

God's plans, like lilies pure

and white unfold;

We must not tear the close-shut

leaves apart,

Time will reveal the chalices of gold.

And if, through patient toil,

We reach the land

Where tired feet with sandals loosed

May rest,

When we shall clearly see

and understand,

I think we will say,

"God knew the best."

What's it Like to be a Christian Mother?

Hannah praying for a son, uttering words to God, words that man cannot understand.

Lord give me soil to cultivate—even though I must water it with tears, and warm it with my own heart's passion. For Heavenly Father, I want to serve you. This material world does not satisfy my soul—my life is like the cold of December; the snows fall, the woods are bare, and North winds wail. The desire for life burns low.

There is a realm where life is real and useful and the pains of duty makes happiness possible. I long to see the water turned to wine, the leper healed, the blind made to see. Lord reveal to me the meaning of the cross and life and death and birth. Let me be a pathway for your purpose. Let me climb from the lowest to the highest—transformed in soul because of giving life to one created in God's image. Brought to this perilous universe; this world of suffering and injustice.

May my rejoicing and my crying be something great in thy sight, and each tear a pearl, a jewel to grace the newly born. Forgetting pain, may the sweet spirit of Mother's love instill in the very substance of my baby's pure and undefiled soul, the love of God.

May I teach him early that someone besides Mother sees his suffering and feels it with him, that his joy and his very being must come to him from a source greater than himself.

A Christian Mother's wholehearted devotion to duty becomes the greatest of pleasure, not for reward or fear of punishment, but for the sake of goodness itself. An instrument of God's will meet with faith and resolution, undaunted and unafraid.

Death for a Christian mother is no defeat. We gaze upon her sleeping face and say "she was a Godly woman."

Her soul returned to its source—the mind of God—like a ripened seed. God reaps whatever value it has brought to him. The tired old body is replaced with a new one; memory retains not the vanished life . The sealed letter is opened; the secret of God's eternity for a Christian mother is read.

"You are a dear daughter and a prize for a minister's wife, and a queen for the mother of my grandsons."

Thank you.

Mother's Day Eve, 1970, after receiving beautiful red and white carnations from my daughter-in-law Joyce.

–Z

Note:

"To search God's word and wisdom find."

This line describes Mom's constant study of scripture. In the days when women were not allowed to "teach men," she taught a large class of men and women at the River Drive Christian Church in Irvine, Kentucky in the late 1940's. This had begun to change in some areas but it was still very unusual in small towns like Irvine.

The minister once told me she was the best Bible teacher he had ever heard.

– John C.

Devotion for a Ladies Class Party

The Bible is our only source of wisdom and knowledge of God. As we meditate upon His word there is a hungering and a thirsting to be like him.

Some Scriptures are plain and easy to be understood but there are others whose meaning does not lie on the surface to be seen at a glance; they require prayerful meditation. Like a miner searching for a precious vein of gold beneath the earth's surface, we search the scriptures . Jesus said of the Old Testament scriptures, "They are that which testify of me."

The Word of God is our guide to all spiritual blessings. The riches of the redeemed are there. There is emancipation from slavery to liberty, transition from darkness to light—from ignorance to knowledge and wisdom. The Bible has things we will never understand.

But God said "Seek and ye shall find, knock and it shall be opened." He has prepared a way for us, so simple a fool can understand. We as humans will never attain the heights of its glory nor fathom its depths, its length is out of our mind's reach. The breadth we knew not but it tends to make it mere fascinating and proves it divine.

The most significant passage contains a shining truth; the more we read it the more we live it until it becomes our very existence.

It is our peace of mind; my peace I give unto you and it is

my food. For he satisfieth my longing soul and filleth the hungry soul with goodness. Our help: He gives us help in the time of trouble for vain is the help of man.

Our shelter, "he shall cover thee with his feathers, under his wings shalt thou trust; his truth shall be thy shield and buckler." Our security: For he shall give his angels charge over thee, to keep thee in all thy ways. God is my reverence; He rules the raging seas, Hallowed be his name.

It was for the love of the truths of this great book that our fathers abandoned their native shore for the wilderness. Let us hold fast to the Bible as an anchor; write its precepts on our hearts and practice them in our lives. To the influence of the Bible we are indebted for all our blessings. Let's make it our guide always. It has civilized nations. It is the one book that can fully lead forth the richest, deepest and sweetest things in the nature of man. Read all other books—philosophy, poetry, history, fiction—but if you would refine the judgment, fertilize the reason. Wing the imagination, attain unto the finest womanhood; read it reverently and prayerfully until its truths have dissolved like iron into the blood.

One of my grandchildren once said to me, "Granny, when you die I am going to see that a Bible is put in your hands in the casket—You wouldn't look like you without it."
I felt complimented!

Without the Bible, man is sailing on a turbulent sea of life without chart or compass, and a shipwrecked life is inevitable. In the Bible man is specifically instructed how to conduct himself in all relationships, conditions and circumstances of life. Individuals and nations that have been guided by this book have been blessed. Righteousness exalteth a nation, but sin is a reproach to any people.

The sun may refuse to shine, the moon cease to reflect light, the stars may fall and the heavens be rolled up like a scroll—the wreck of matter and the crash of worlds may come and the judgment day be set, but when the angel of the Lord shall descend on pinions dipped in the love light enveloping the throne of God, and planting one foot upon the land and one upon the sea, and shall declare that "time shall be no more." Even then the Church of Christ shall stand secure as the throne of God itself. The word of our God shall stand forever.

Ladies Sunday School lesson
River Drive Christian Church
Irvine, Kentucky
Date unknown

Heaven, the City of God

II Corinthians 5:1 "For we know that if our earthly house of this tabernacle were dissolved, we have a building of God. An house not made with hands, eternal in the heavens."

Acts 3:19,20,21 "Repent ye therefore, and be converted that your sins may be blotted out, when the times of refreshing shall come from the presence of the Lord."

The soul is without adventure that has no longing to see that city four square whose gates are of pearl and streets are of gold. One has no sense of imagination if he has no desire to be with God and walk beside that pure river that makes glad the city of God. The whole family of Heaven and the redeemed from earth will be united around the throne in glorious fellowship with God the Father, Christ the Son and the Holy Spirit and all the host of God's Heaven.

The sunshine of His smile the supreme glory of Heaven's great depths of light known only to the Spirit of Light. And to gaze on the face of God the creator, the architect of Heaven and earth and to breath the holy incense of love there forever good without fear of evil, life without the dread of death, pleasure without pain, music without discord.

What an awakening for the righteous.

Daniel 12:2 "And many of them that sleep in the dust of the earth, shall awake, some to everlasting life and some to shame and everlasting contempt."

Job 14:12 "So man lieth down and riseth not, till the heavens be no more, they shall not awake, nor be raised out of their sleep."

Corinthians 5:1 "For we know that if our earthly house of this tabernacle be dissolved we have a house not made with hands eternal in the heavens."

The Spirit

Greater than all of earth's riches,
Than the heaven with its numberless stars,
More powerful than mighty waves of the ocean,
Or the greatness for which men aspire.

More desirable than the gold of Ophir,
Yet as gentle as a light South wind,
It reveals the greatest of kingdoms,
It's the Holy Spirit within.

It unites our soul with our master,
The fruit that it bears is love.
Quench not the spirit of Jesus,
Once received in the form of a dove.

Our eyes cannot behold it,
Our ears cannot hear its voice.
The heart hath not fathomed its mystery,
But in it God's people rejoice.

They stand like the rock of ages,
Though at them fiery darts may be hurled.
People of the world cannot receive it,
For God's kingdom is not of this world.

Footprints on the Sands of Time

Do you read the Bible daily?
Heed the signs along the way—
Are you sure you are on the right road?
Caution brother, watch and pray.

He'll direct you at the crossroads,
On your path his light will shine.
Walking in his steps you're leaving
Footprints on the sands of time.

There's no parking, keep on going;
Dangerous curves please keep in mind.
He will lead you through the darkness
If you heed the Gospel sign.

In the valley or on the mountain
It matters not how steep the climb.
When He sees your teardrops falling
He will slip His hand in thine.

I Will be Waiting

Son, when you come I will be waiting,
As I have so many times before.
I'll greet you with a smile
That hides my heartaches.

Yes, when you come, I'll be waiting at the door.
And when my earthly tasks are finished,
And I am living in paradise on another shore,
I'll still be there to greet you.

Darling, with Jesus I'll be waiting at the door.
You have always come when duty called you,
Never given grief to parents' hearts,
Only pleasant memories we have about you.
Some day, sweet day, again we'll never part.

His Voice

I heard His voice
In the newborn boy's cry;
In the sigh of the saint
when he came to die.
I heard His voice
In the morning fair;
Again when my burden
He helped me bear.
I heard His voice
In the sadness of night;
When a sinner repented
And saw the light.
I heard His voice
When hope seemed gone,
When I stood on the brink
Helpless and alone.
I heard His voice
And courage came,
With hope and love
His Spirit remained.

Tired

Tired of sifting the false
from the true,
Tired of wondering
just what I should do.
Careful of "being" what I should be
So that others may speak well of me.

Tired of smiling when I want to weep.
Of giving to others what I want to keep.
Tired of guarding the words I speak.
Tired, just tired; my spirit, just weak.

Lord lift me up from this selfish tomb
And take me to your upper room
That I may consecrate life anew
And walk alone, dear God, with you.
Please fill my cup with rich, red wine,
The passion of your heart pour into mine.

My strength renew.

Just Me

Yes, I know this busy life will end,
This body back to earth will blend.
These tired hands will be at rest,
Gently folded on my breast.
But today I have a heart, a mind
To search God's word and wisdom find.
As men and women long ago
Through years of toil sought to know,
They suffered pain for many years,
Their bodies bathed in blood and tears.
They found a destiny sublime,
That I pray, shall too be mine.
A faith I have that all is true,
These eyes will vision Heaven, too,
My heart knows not the human creeds
But love performs such noble deeds.
Just me, just risen from the sod,
To see the radiant land and God.

My Greatest Desire

Oh! God—let thy greatness shine in my innermost soul till the thoughts of self pass away. This temple, Lord, is thine, make it a holy temple. Erase all thoughts that lead astray or cause neglect of thy greatness.

Let me feel the ecstasy of love for Thee. And when thou takest back the soul that you hast given, oh, may it be with thee in Heaven.

Help me to go on loving, even though the love I crave in others be silent. Let me be dead to myself and my unhappy thoughts, that I may find all my glory in thy greatness. Thou art love, and thou art power—lift me up, lest I stumble on the stones, in the midst of doubt and thoughts that honor thee not, your will is my greatest of all desires and the surest of all triumphs.

Cast me not off in the time of old age;
Forsake me not when my strength faileth.

The Gospel

The Gospel is relevant to every generation.
The methods of preaching may change
but the Gospel remains the same.
In the thinking of the great apostle Paul,
the prime need of the Macedonians
was the Gospel.
He never planned to get involved in
"slum clearance" or ghetto problems.
No, God sent Paul to preach the Gospel.
He was not disobedient
to the heavenly vision.
The Gospel unmixed with doctrines,
theories, and commandments of men,
is what the world needs.
It is as relevant now
as it was first proclaimed at Pentecost.

Note:

As you may have noticed from her writings, Mom talked about death and heaven a lot. The last time I spoke to her she was in the hospital and we were all expecting her to be released by the next day at the latest. As I was leaving her room she said:

> *"If I am not here when you get back, remember, that's just the cycle of life."*

Those were the last words I ever heard her say; she died that night from a heart attack.

– John C.

Home at Last

When the sun has gone down
        on the last day of my life,
and I have entered death's dark portals.
There swings wide the
        Golden Gate of Life,
There comes the call
        and my trembling lips reply:
        "Lord here I am."

I awake to the daybreak of a new eternity.
How can I describe the heavenly vision with earthly words?
I will hear a whisper "my beloved is mine."
I will lean on His bosom and
        with His precious nail scarred hand
        He will wipe away the last cold tears of death.
I will look and behold Him as He is.
I won't be looking through the glass dimly,
        but face to face He will be there
        and I will have no need of prayer.

Radiant bliss, and eternal happiness
        Home, home at last.

Her Nature

God Made All things Beautiful

The big bright yellow harvest moon;
The sweet scent of a rose in bloom;
The beauty of the stars that glow;
Mountain summits topped with snow.
The upturned earth of virgin sod,
Like a white page from the book of God.
April blue in a pair of wings,
Magic song the song bird sings,
But of all beautiful things bringing joy
Is the simple smile of a little boy.

The Moon

On nights like this
When the big round moon
Smiles down on me
And lights my room
I am not lonely.
For the while
I talk to God and
I hear Him smile,
Then all the burdens
of the day
Just fold themselves
And hide away.

Zona was a trained and natural 'care-giver'

God's Handiwork

So close to the road's impurity
Where feet of men may trod
A little bit of common clay
Was formed in the image of God.
The timid pulse, the faltering breath,
Became triumphant from the sod.
In man God breathed an immortal soul;
Man is the handiwork of God.

Psalm 91:11–12
October 21, 1969

Finished Art

I am tired tonight
I am weary
I long for my rest and sleep.
Tomorrow I'll finish my work, son;
I will do something for you to keep.
But that night when slumber
O'er took me
The task was finished by him.
When I awoke next morning
I thought my work a priceless gem!
I was old and tired
But I tried
And he gave it the finishing touch.
But he never wounded my pride
And the kingdom of Heaven is such.
He kept it all a secret,
That he had finished the art,
I gloried in what I'd accomplished—
He cherished it in his heart.

The Rainbow

There is a beauty in the rainbow,
        that the heart cannot resist
Radiant in the Eastern heavens
        in the early morning mist.

It is a mercy sign of promise,
        God's covenant to man
That this world won't be destroyed
        by a mighty flood again.

Seven colors; red binds them all together,
        And thus bound, they form a perfect bow.
Hence, we think of the blessed Savior
        Since for us He allowed His blood to flow.

Yellow, so pale and delicate,
        as leaves in the Autumn rain,
Represents hope that springs eternal
        that the soul will live again.

Pale blue melts into the yellow,
        intermingled until both are one.
Faith like the blue of heavens;
        hope in the power of His son.

Light blue expresses faith and courage,
        Indigo is the darker shade
When faith might grow weak or falter,
        And God keeps us unafraid.

Tucked between the red and yellow,
    'tis orange, the child of love,
Matured in hope and ready to bear fruit
    for Heaven up above.

Hope and faith have united
    with breath of leaves of green,
So restful like the peace of the forest
    o'er all the bow may be seen.

The yellow seems to have faded,
    for hope isn't needed now,
With the Royal purple robes of the Master,
    hope has fulfilled her vow.

Perfectly blend all colors together;
    the answer you get is white,
We stand in the presence of the Holy,
    purified in His sight.

We kneel in adoration
    before God's throne above.
For the rainbow around our Savior
    Is the promise of God's love.

The Hills

I was born in the hills—
In the hills I found faith,
In the hills I found peace,
In the hills I found God.
I left the beautiful hills—
Where I had found faith,
Where I had found God,
Where I had found love.
If I ascend to heaven, He is there.
If I make my bed in hell, behold Thou art there.
If I take the wings of the morning
And dwell in the uttermost parts of the sea,
Even there shall thy hand hold me.
If I say "surely the darkness shall cover me,
Even the night shall be light about me.
Yea the darkness hideth not from thee,
But the night shineth as the day.
Darkness and light are both alike to Thee."

When I am awake I am still with Thee oh, God.

Little Boy Fishing

A little boy played and dreamed one day,
As he fished in a little stream.
He played and fished alone one day
And no one knew his dream.
The sun went down behind the hill,
Twilight began to fall.
But he fished and dreamed until
He heard his mother's call.
His old dog Shep restless grew
And barked while he tugged at his sleeve.
Though his dreaming day was over
He was reluctant to leave.
No one knew the thoughts of the lad
As he sat with fishing pole,
But today he's still fishing though he is a man,
His reward: the saving of souls.
Yet no one knows the dreams he dreams
As he holds his fishing rod.
Fishing for souls in the stream of life
And his bait is the word of God.
Yet his heart still loves the song of the stream,
This fisherman of men.
But now his heart of love casts out this net
—The word of God—again and again!

Love Is

Were you there when one planet,
much brighter than the others,
shed its heavenly light above the Child of Bethlehem?
Asleep in a manger where a Virgin Mother
watched and breathed the secrets of his birth in
whispered prayer to God alone, with love far above a
Mother's love for the child God had placed in her
mother care?

A mother, a wife in God's plan must remain what God
has ordained them to be—a mother. A wife.
No more, no less.
Her name: Love.

And what is love?

Love is
a crown where warm blood flows on a willing brow.
Love is
to keep on keeping on, until the hand of God is found
and His divine spirit reaches your soul and purifies.
Love is
music like the waves of Hallelujahs that angels set to
music and rang out among the golden stars until one
star pointed and led souls to the Christ child.

Love is

tenderness and kindness that children show to their aged parents.

Love is

the tears of lonely parents when children forget them. Not in pity for themselves, but for the child with a hardened heart.

Love is

a poor man's hut where the blessings of God are sought and granted.

Love is

a vow at the marriage altar.

Love is

a Father's calloused hands.

Love is

a Mother in the small dark hours of night, watching bedside of a sick child.

In life's darkest hours of gloom, love brings a bouquet of roses with the thorns removed. When God opens His arms and accepts our prayers.

God is love.

The Old Fireplace

It was like a sanctuary
After Daddy's evening grace
When from the table we assembled
Around the old fireplace.
Someone always stirred the embers
Until the flames leapt forth with light,
And we felt so warm and cozy
From the dark chills of the night.
Pleasant memories of those evenings
Father time cannot erase,
When we shared our joys and heartaches
Around that old fireplace.
They were kind and gentle people,
Can't evaluate their worth;
They knew more about the heaven
Than they knew about the earth.
Then came days of separation;
There were tears on every face.
But the faith will live forever
Taught around that old fireplace.

This is the chimney of their fireplace at Wagersville

Historical note:
the door is where Joyce killed John C.'s cat before they were dating, but that's another story not included in this book.

I Remember Canyon Falls

I remember the Falls and the canyon
And the legend that lingers there.
How the spring at the base of Bear Wallow
Was the bathing place for the bear.
I loved the sweet breath of morning,
The mountain laurel kissed by the dew,
The path where in childhood I lingered
To gaze on its great scenic view.
Engraved on the walls of my memory
Are the hemlock, holly and pine,
In all their majestic grandeur
Made the essence of life seem divine.
The song of the falling waters
As the seasons would come and go.
The mystery thrill of the legend
That I heard in the firelight's glow.
I remember the falls and the canyon;
The most beautiful place on earth,
For there was the home of my childhood,
There was the place of my birth.

One of the 'Falls'
near Beattyville, Kentucky

I Have Heard What I Have Listened For

The gurgling of brooks, the warbling of birds,
The whispering of wind in the pines.
The voices of nature
        in the twilight hour,
The friendly bark of a dog,
The purring of a kitten, the echo of childish laughter
        resounding o'er the hill.
The sound of the chimes,
The song of the saints,
        the mountain top sermons.
Pledges of love, confessions of faith.
The voice of the Spirit, "Go in peace,"
        words of the Master.
"Though your sins be as scarlet,
They shall be as white as snow."
        I have heard
                what I listened for,
                        and found what I searched for,
                                and seen what I looked for.

The Old Gang

There's a scrapbook in my keepsakes.
I read it o'er again
Leafing through memory's pages.
There's a page from lover's lane.
    There was Clara, Gail and Helen,
    Also Sandy, Bill and Ken.
Wonder what has happened to them.
Many years gone by since then.
The happy hours of lovers.
We shall never live again;
    Clara, Gail and Helen,
    Sandy, Bill and Ken.
There's an old tree in the canyon
Where we carved our lover's names.
And our initial there beside them,
Oh how sweet was love's first flame,
    For Clara, Gail and Helen,
    Sandy, Bill and Ken.

I would love to see the old gang;
Many years gone by since then.

I Found God

I listened in the silence
For the sound of his dear feet
But I heard them in the tumult
And the turmoil on the street.
In the mud and scum of things
The fairest lily grows,
And you'll find the smile of God
Not only on the rose.

It's Time to be Happy

When we see the lightening
And hear the thunder roll,
We know the God of the storm
Is also the God of the soul.
It's time to be happy.
We planned our lives
We dreamed our dreams
When we were young,
By a beautiful stream.
It was time to be happy.
On the mountain high
And on the cleft
We saw the signs
The flood had left.
It was time to be happy
When we see God's hand
In the flickering stars,
People see God in our lives
As they are.
Although in life there is Always pain.
We have God's promise; we'll meet again.

It's time to be happy.

July 4th, 1977

April

I am a child of April,
        I love the violet sprinkled sod.
The song birds' mighty music,
        The organs of my God.
(My reflection is in the puddles)
        I have no hurts or fears,
I see waters by the road side
        Where April weeps her tears.
Her tears of rejoicing.

        It's apple blossom time;
Their fragrance bring a sweetness
        Of joy divine.
Oh, April is a miracle.
        God gave me eyes to see
The beautiful of all the life
        That April gave to me.

The Summer Is Ended

The asters bloom
And the crickets sing
The shadows grow long
And the leaves begin to fall.
Yes, the summer is over,
And souls are unsaved *(Jeremiah 8:20).*
But around the little country church,
There were showers of blessings.
Times when our trembling feet
Seem to be standing on holy ground.
A time of refreshing,
A time when the servant of God
Appeared to be a minister of miracles.
Yet he went away sad,
Still calling his lost sheep.

Oh, Jerusalem, Jerusalem,
How often would I have gathered
Thee under my wings.
But ye would not!
(Luke 13:34)

Life's Treasures

Watching stars on a balmy night;
    Seeing the wild geese in their annual flight;
A beautiful rainbow after the shower,
    The lights of home in the Vesper hour.

My mother's smiling, soft brown eyes.
    My daddy's songs of paradise.
These are the things fond memory holds
    Buried very deep like a chest of gold.

The swaying pines in the wind and storm,
    Holding my babies in my arms;
The confidence of a friend in need,
    The joy of performing a Christ-like deed.

Feeding the hungry, both body and soul;
    Helping to make the sick ones whole;
To ride with my companion on a moonlit night;
    And watch the moonbeams shining and bright.

I love the Indian Summer's days,
    The colored leaves and autumn haze,
Thanksgiving when the Grand ones come,
    The turkey dinner, and the children home.

A childish voice loud and clear;
    Calling, "Granny! Granny! We are all here."
Some of the things that life has given,
    That makes me know the taste of Heaven.

To ride horse-back in a misty rain,
    Or hear the whistle of a far away train.
To read poetry on a rainy day;
    Or baby-sit while children play.

To watch a cake turning brown in the oven;
    Or watch young lovers with their cooin' and lovin'.
But the one thing nearest to heaven with me;
    Is to be in Church with all my family.

1959

His Voice

I have loved the stars too fondly
To be fearful of the night.
I have trusted all to Jesus
And I know he leads me right.
I have found his voice in the thunder,
When the storm was wild and high,
When the raging sweeping waters
Covered all the earth and sky.
When the sound was loud and angry,
It revealed his wondrous power.
Even the darkest moments
Can become God's Holy power.
I heard his voice in the desert
Amid the absence of all sound.
The very silence of the centuries
Made it seem like holy ground.
Then I heard his voice in a dew drop
As it sparkled on the rose
And it soothed my soul to slumber
Restful sleep—a sweet repose.

July 1960

When

The fringes of the sunset;
    The rose burst of the dawn,
The tide of the years
    Keeps surfing on and on.
Yesterday there was purpose
    Life had treasures hidden deep
But time and tide aren't waiting
    The years we cannot keep.
It grieves my heart, and I wonder
    But I cannot see for tears
When did I grow old?
    When were my aging years?

My Garden

Sanctify my garden, Lord,
And let me not forget
That every green and living thing
Proves Thou art ruler yet.
And may the sweet bloom of each flower
Unto my soul proclaim
The heavenly beauty of Thy power
The greatness of Thy name.
Some plants are not so healthy Lord
They cause my heart much grief,
My hands are bleeding from the thorns
Left by the withering leaf.
Please hush my tears
And give me faith
As I kneel on waiting sod,
And let my lips whisper courage
To lift their heads to God.

Zona was a natural in nature, circa 1920

Her Sundry Thoughts

If All the World Could Laugh

If all the world could laugh,
Together for one day,
All wars would cease
And clouds of doubt
Silently melt away.

If all the world could laugh
In friendly brotherhood,
The stones would roll away
Triumphant rise the good.

If all the world could laugh,
There'd surely be joy in Heaven
All hearts be happy and free,
And peace on earth be given.

–January, 1975

With Apologies to Kipling

When her last poem is written
And the ink from her pen is dry
She will rest and I know she will need it
And I no longer will have to lie.

I sure hope that she will be happy
When she climbs those golden, stairs.
And I hope they won't be embarrassed
When she tries to write poetry there.

I'm afraid when she gets rested,
Say perhaps an aeon or two,
She'll rise and again start writing
But I guess they'll know what to do.

Some people mess up the choir
Because they've not voices to sing,
But Mother, with her it's different
To her poetry she ever will cling.

Ha–Ha Kipling.

–Z

New Year

Cover the embers,
        Turn out the light
Bid farewell to the old year
        That is dying tonight.
Rich were the garners
        Its summit attained,
Like a battle well fought,
        And a guerdon gained.
Precious the summer
        And sermons we've heard,
Revivals of saints,
        And feasts of His word.
Sharp were its thorns
        And scarred are our feet,
But they passed,
        And their music is sweet.
Gone with its weaving
        Of silver and gold,
It's joys and its heartaches,
        Like a tale that's been told.
Cover the embers,
        That once glowed so bright,
God's reservoir of goodness,
        Grants a New Year tonight.

Mind-blowing

When I woke up this morning
I felt I'd lost my head.
I put my clothes on–
then pulled them off–
then went right back
to bed.

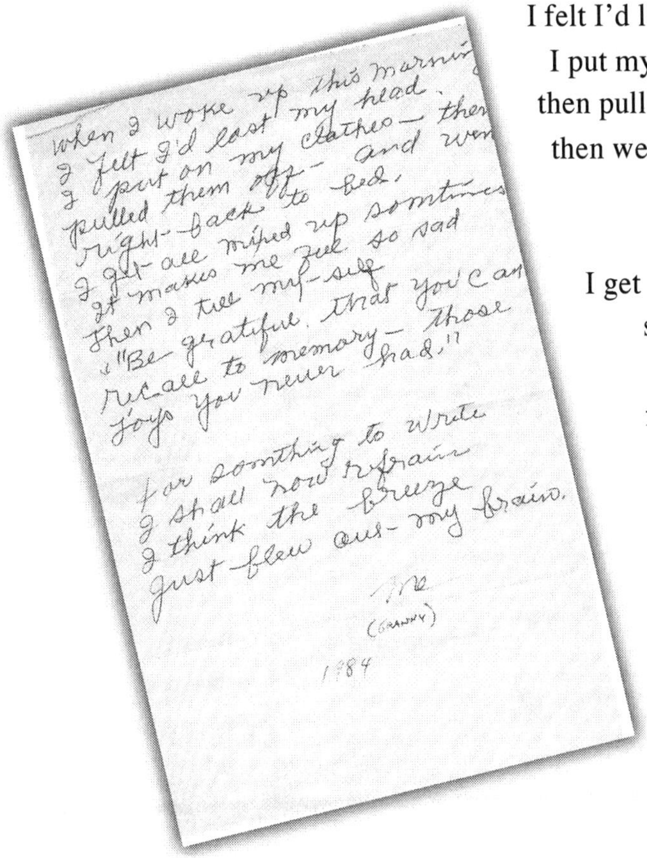
when I woke up this mornin
I felt I'd lost my head.
I put on my clothes – then
pulled them off – and wen
right back to bed.
I get all mixed up somtimes
It makes me feel so sad
Then I tell my-self
"Be grateful that you can
recall to memory – those
joys you never had."

For somthing to write
I shall now refrain
I think the breeze
Just blew out my brain.

Me
(Granny)

1984

I get all mixed-up
sometimes—
It makes me
feel so sad—
Then I tell
myself,
"Be grateful
that you can
recall to
memory
those
joys you
never had."

For something to write I shall now refrain.
I think the breeze Just blew out my brain.

1984

Vivid Memories of Thirty Years Ago

After church we motored over to College Hill

to see the Gravitts.

No one home.
The old Shepherd dog came out wagging his tail,
Seemed he was saying "well get out and come in."

We just drove slow and viewed the old home
where happiness once lived.

We thought about ;
three boys in overalls
a dog named Shep
a cat named Mergertroid
and a mare named Pill-Due.
The best neighbors we ever had.
Evenings making ice cream
with the Willoughbys.

For awhile we just forgot that everyone was gone
and strangers were there now.

But it was nice to see the dogwoods;
the red buds
the tulips
and the green, green, grass
of our once beloved home.

Our richest blessings
are the precious memories God has granted.

Most of my life now consists of memories.
My three score years and nine are gone.
Just one more year and I shall have
lived my allotted time.

Seems like a dream, yet it's been a pleasant dream.
I came, I saw, I conquered.

I came as an infant crying in the night.
I came crying for the light.
In a Christian home with tender care
Loving hearts I found were there.

I Came—
I saw the beginning of my years
I saw my joy mixed with my tears

I Saw—

I felt the pangs of worldly strife
I saw the mystic love of life.

I Conquered—
I fought the fight, the victory I achieved

I sought forgiveness from the Father.
I have grieved.

I conquered.

Little Clock

O' little clock I think you're great
You never shirk or hesitate.
Constantly your hands move on,
A day is born, a day is gone.
You say to me, "No trouble borrow,
My hands are pointing to tomorrow."
Then, when my heart is gay and sings,
You tell me time has pretty wings
That fly so fast across the day,
To not forget it's time to pray.

January 15, 1968

Humility

I despaired because my soul was hungry
Until I met a man who had no appetite.
And when I shared with him my bread from heaven
He was made whole and my soul was satisfied.
I ask my God for better understanding,
And then one day I met a fool.
With pity then I prayed To God for mercy,
On him who never knew my school.

January 15, 1969

Heart-cleaning

Just been cleaning up today. Or at least I made a start,
To put things in order; to clean out my heart.
Been saving up for years and years, so I thought today
I'd take a general cleaning, and throw a lot away.
I had so many useless things, to clutter up the space,
Sometimes for new and better things I could hardly find a place.
There was a bowl of scraps, like anger and doubt,
And old sore spots of grudge and hurts.
So I gathered up the clutter and pitched the whole mess out
And in the space they'd laid, I found some treasures there—
A Mother's dream, a baby's kiss, antiques so bright and rare,
And a heart so full of treasure when the trash was cleared away.
And now that I have made a start, I'll heart-clean every day.

Courageous

What a beautiful scene in the dawn's early light;
Those moon pioneers make a thrilling splash down.
The nation thrills at their accomplishing act—the thing the world thought could never be accomplished. Even old glory spread herself so proudly—every star and every stripe seemed to be saying *welcome home from your orbit around the moon*—the most sensational adventure man has yet made. The breathless moment, the anxious days and nights of prayerful waiting.

But oh, say can you see by the dawn's early light those volunteers for orbit, those pioneers that have dedicated their lives to God's son from outer space who came to redeem this world from sin. They too are burning through the air; they too have a pinpoint landing—but how many red carpets are being laid?

How many bands are playing?
How many messages of encouragement
from the dignitaries of the land?

But God knows of their bravery and someday he will pin the medals on their breasts. For He knows, and He is able to keep what is committed unto him against that day.
That day of landing—of slash down—God bless and keep you forever near him.

December 29, 1968

Adventure

Adventure carried me far above the world;
My ship into the outer space was hurled.
But disaster struck without the slightest sign.
It was then I learned that faith and hope were mine.
I learned to use these qualities, before unused.
Perhaps in hurried days, I had this power abused.
I learned the thing that man must learn, alone!
The great adventure man can know is
Power in God, and not his own.

Zona, circa 1940

The Lame

As I walked the pilgrim journey,
With limbs so strong and young,
A comrade walked beside me
Who had been lame for so long.
I could have journeyed faster,
The prize of life to claim,
But the one who walked beside me
Was slow, for he was lame.

When I came to life's deep waters,
I called upon the Lord.
He said, "One walks beside you
Help him across the ford."
The burdens of life grew heavy,
And the way for me seemed dim,
But the Master's voice spoke plainly;
"Have you considered him?"
For what you have done for others
That is what you've done for me,
So I helped my lame companion;
Together we crossed life's sea.

June 10, 1970

Saturday Night

Cool breezes, children on bikes,
Hubby listening to a ball game—
Life on HALLS LANE.

Hippies walking down the street
almost nude, and dirty.
Baby waving at me, smiling.
A German police dog guarding
a child on a bike.

Spot sleeping in the cool grass.
Another tiny dog yapping to get inside the house.

Neighbor's grand-baby seriously ill in the hospital,
and the next house up the lane—the husband
in hospital with a stroke.

Night is falling—It's lonesome.

June 28, 1975

Wait 'til My Ship Comes In

He toiled along 'neath storm and sun,
Seemed his tasks were never done.
But he'd throw back his shoulders
And say with a grin,
    "Just you wait till my ship comes in."
But the days of his youth were passing away,
And his tasks were harder day after day.

He would smile and manage a feeble grin,
    "Sure wish my ship would come in."
The time has come—his shoulders are bent
The best of his years already spent,
But no banners are flying.
He fails to grin;
    "My ship has gone down—she's not coming in!"

But far away, a speck on the sea,
    "My ship! My ship! is coming to me.
    She is not laden with silver and gold,
    Treasures are mine to have and to hold.
    I never knew how I could win,
    That's my ship—she's coming in."

Laden with memories of a family
As happy a bunch as ever you'll see.
He had toiled and given the best he had,
His reward is love for hubby and dad.
A sigh of happiness, and a grin,
    "I guess sure enough, my ship has come in!"

War

I looked for you
When spring brought apple blossoms.
Then when the sickle reaped the summer grain.
    You never came when autumn winds were blowing
    Nor when the icy breath of winter came.
I watched little white clouds
Sailing in the moon light
Like little ships searching for the shore.
I saw the mail man slowly pass my mail box,
    I knew you wouldn't write
    Or come home any more.
Now I walk a lonely road
With just a memory,
Of happy hours before the war,
    That changed my life
    and brought these chilling heart aches.
The message read...
    ...no
    ...no.
I cannot repeat those cruel words again.

What is Mother's Love?

It is a gentle smile
    A tender embrace
A child's dream
    Of an angel's face.
It's a star that shines
    On the darkest night,
It's a soft warm hand
    Leading to the light
It's a tonic for all
    When they are in doubt
It's a place to run to
    When school is out.
It's a guide to youth
    A rod to reprove wrong
A haven of rest
    When the day is too long.

NOTE:

Mother is describing the home-place that I remember. There was a swing in the orchard suspended on log legs, and hills on either side with a stream flowing nearby from a mountain spring. Stretching out behind the house was a long meadow. "Around the hill" was where her older married sister lived, Alice, the mother of my cousin Carmel..

– John C.

The Little Girl I Used to Be

The little girl I used to be, she visits me tonight.
She seems so strange and innocent,
of what is wrong or right.
A little soul so white and clean, a voice so true and sweet,
She came through the blossoming meadow;
I see the sparkling dew drops on her feet.

She has a wreath of flowers, gathered on the mountain side,
while she thought and sang of angels
and the stars where angels hide.
Today she played in the meadow;
tomorrow will be near the spring.
Someday she will climb the mountain
where the trailing arbutus cling.
The swing near the trees in the orchard
with thoughts of God and what He gives
And the path over around the hill,
where dear Aunt Phebia lives.

Little girl you comfort me for my heart is tired and old.
I've carried my burdens in-the heat of the day
and felt the bitterness of the cold.
So long ago and far away, this little girl I knew,
But to her dreams and all her plans
I find my heart's been true.

A Happy Day

I will not pine for a day that's gone
As the evening sun descends,
Time takes her toll and marches on
Taking our loved ones and our friends.
She takes away the bloom of youth
And leaves us void of health,
Reveals to us the simple truth
That riches are better than wealth.
Yes, I have been rich—I walked with a child
and taught him the Saviors' will.
I have been more than blessed,
I saw him smile
When his soul with Christ was filled

Not only one but many more
I helped along the way,
I will not pine as the sun goes down
For I've had a happy day.

February 13, 1968

I Have Learned

One shattered hope is not the end;
I'll build new dreams
And make new friends.
I've had heartaches
Through the years
But I've learned lessons
Through my tears.
The stars above the tempest gleam;
One disappointment is not
The end of dreams.

Mother's Tomb

"They said, if I came here I would find her,"
In his eyes there were no tears,
For he had grown free from emotion
His heart had grown hard through the years.

"Yes, that is my darling Mother;
I should have been by her side.
She seemed so lonely and frightened
and clung to me when Dad died.
I guess I left it to others
To do what she wanted done.
They must have felt as I did,
and Mother died alone.
I guess it was her loneliness
That took her away so soon.
For Dad went away in December
Now Mother is gone in June.

I'd pray, but I have forgotten
Just what she taught me to say.
Oh, Mother come back from that echoless shore,
And teach me again to pray."

Then the flood of his tears started flowing.
And he prayed in his mother's room.
For he prayed and received forgiveness
At the foot of his mother's tomb.

– 1968

Note:

We know that this is not about Mom's own mother, but we also know it describes the circumstances of someone she knew. Exactly who that was is something that Mom took to her own grave.

– John C.

You Live Your Life

You live your life
And I'll live mine.
And may your burdens be lighter.
Because our lives
Touched each other today,
The world to me has grown brighter.

You plant your garden
And I'll plant mine
And we'll work through sunny weather.
But if your garden fails
And my garden blooms,
We'll share the flowers together.

You live in your house
And I'll live in mine
Across the street from each other,
Let's be neighbors,
not strangers, friend–
That way we can help one another.

Oh Where is My Flock?

Oh where is my flock?
My beautiful flock
That I tended with loving care?
Who scattered my sheep?
Where are my lambs?
I am searching, but they are not there.
Are they on the mountains?
The hills wild and bare?
Are they sheltered in another fold?
Oh Father, are my little ones
In your care?
Or are they perishing in the cold?
I did not forsake
My beautiful flock,
I was wounded and driven away.
In other green pastures
I have feasted my soul
But I mourn for my flock today.

This was written in memory of the labors of Harold Deitch
at the First Christian Church in Irvine, Kentucky
during the late 1940s and early 1950s.

–Z

Her Lambs

When her lambs in the fold were sleeping
At the end of the toilsome day,
On her knees I heard her weeping,
"Keep them Lord; don't let them stray.
Time will bring many changes,
And my lambs will go away."
So earnestly I hear her pleading.
"Keep them Lord; don't let them stray."
Always her lambs—always her mission
As she toils through the tiresome day.
Yet her thoughts are with her children,
"Keep them Lord; don't let them stray."
When her tired soul is leaving—
Her tired body made of clay—
I will listen for her last words,
"Keep them Lord; don't let them stray."

Are All the Children In?

"Are all the children in?"
I heard the mother say.
"This is the vesper hour,
Soon the end of day.
Are all the children in?
My eyes have grown so dim
I cannot search in twilight;
I'll leave the search to Him.
Are all the children in?
Oh, shepherd seek and find
If one has gone astray,
For I am old and blind.
Are all the children in?
Oh, shepherd bring them to the fold,
I cannot sleep tonight
If one is in the cold."

October 1972

Average Saturday Night Sermon

Lord, it is Saturday night, and I haven't had time to prepare a sermon for the morning service. I wonder...

Let me look through my files—oh mmm, yeah, here is a good one I used six months ago. They never heard it then. The older ones were mostly asleep and the youth seem interested only in each other. So they won't recognize it—I am sure. Well, here is Deacon Webb and Sister Sutton, but Lord, they know the Bible so much better than I do there is no use trying to meet with their approval.

I guess that's taken care of... I'11 just turn on tv and watch a Saturday night movie. I really am tired, that was a real game of golf today. Ol' Bill sure hates for me to beat him.

I really ought to try to get up a different sermon. The movie isn't interesting, I'll just turn it off and think awhile.

What did I do this week anyway?

Monday I took Old man Duff fishing, he had been pestering me for a year to go fishing with him.

Then Tuesday I had a headache didn't get up until noon. The youth group came over in the afternoon and we played ball.

Wednesday I went to the hospital to see if any of the church members were there. They weren't.

Thursday I called on Miss Jones. That old maid—if she don't get a little more generous with her money, I'm going to quit calling on her.

Friday I rested. It's a poor church that can't let the preacher have one day a week for his own.

People at church seem indifferent nowadays—

What is that sermon title??

Yes, "He shall reward every Man according to his works." *(Matthew l6:27)*

Note:

I have heard Mother talk about a certain 'Mr. Wilson' whom we saw once when we were in town, and she confided in me that he had been a youthful suitor. He may be the object of this poem, which she wrote when she was just seventeen years old.

Dad was the strong silent type; faithful, hard-working, frugal, honest, and at times funny, but I don't remember him telling Mother that he loved her, nor do I recall seeing him embrace her.

– John C.

Shattered Love

Ruby red and diamond bright,
	Glistening in the cold moonlight,
Due to anger, due to pride,
	Here is the place where our love died.

In the silence cold as snow,
	Where did shattered pieces go?
Treasures lying at our feet,
	Do not touch, they pierce, they cheat.

Ghosts by day and ghosts by night,
	Scattered in the cold moonlight.
Ghosts of passing, ghosts of pride;
	Haunting ghosts where our love died.

December 1919

Rambling Rose

The heart that I gave you
And then took away,
In the twilight of life
Is still aching today.

I still have your picture,
Sweet love of our teens,
I'm the one who was cruel;
I was jealous and mean.

Yes, I wed another,
As the story goes,
But the one I most wanted
Was my "sweet Rambling Rose."

I asked you my darling
To be my own wife,
You said you were "too young"
for the duties of life.

This little picture of you,
Hidden all these long years,
I am free now to gaze on,
But I can't for the tears.

Courtships are sweet and dreamy thresholds of
unseen temples that pass on–but never return–
like ships that pass in the night.

–Z

Why?

Since I caught a vanished moment
of your love through passing years,
I am wondering why you're silent,
As love should conquer every fear.
I never dreamed your heart was throbbing
With a love you didn't show.
Why not let your heart reveal it
In the days of long ago?

Sweet Dream of Bliss

I saw you again in my dream last night,
We threw back the curtain of years.
You held me so tight and my heart was so light;
But only in dreams are you near.

Will you come to me in my dreams again
and touch my hand and my heart?
Together in dreamland we're happy, sweetheart,
In dreamland, we don't have to part.

You laughed again like you used to do
And my lips felt the thrill of your kiss.
The angels were watching my dreams and so
They granted a sweet dream of bliss.

We talked of the days when we were in love
and we traveled down old lovers lane,
I prayed in my dream to heaven above
We would never leave dreamland again.

When Angels Took a Holiday

When the angels took a holiday
They left you all alone,
I found you in the garden
Where the Honeysuckle bloom.

Chorus:
How could I resist the sweetest kiss
That I had ever known,
When the angels took a holiday
and left you all alone.

I hope they will forgive me
For taking you away;
I found my bit of heaven
When they took their holiday.

I knew my fate was something great,
True happiness was my own
When the angels took a holiday
And left you all alone.

–Chappie

Note: When she was thinking of a verse as a song,
Mom would use "Chappie" as her nom de plume.

– John C.

NOTE:

Mothers' evening routine in my childhood would be to gather her three boys around her and read from the Bible and then pray for each one of us. Vivid memories of winter evenings with a fire in the fireplace—our only source of heat from when I was age six through nine.

– John C.

Twilight

Twilight is falling, and I hear voices of loved ones, over on the other side of the river. It isn't far away—in youth that golden land of love seemed many miles away.

But now it is evening; the long weary day will soon be over. So I walk on hallowed ground and listen to heavenly music, and my thoughts are sacred thoughts; the things of the world grow dim and are almost past. I care not for them.

I hear the Master's voice; he calls the children and I sit at his feet and listen, and wait—are they coming? Will they find the way? And faith hovers over the ribbon of darkness falling in the twilight. And love presses hard against my heart.

Then I fall on my knees in the thickening darkness and I pray. O' God, watch over my little flock and keep them in the fold. When my labors are over I commit them into thy keeping.

God save my people, for Jesus sake.

Amen.

February 14, 1974

A Wave for the Road

There's an old, old house near the big highway,
Where sits an old man day by day.
He waves his hand to everyone
and smiles at each as they pass along.

Pathetic and lonely he seems to be,
But passing by you're sure to see Him
Wave his hand to everyone and smile
each time as they pass along.

In the old, old house by the side of the road,
He has been a friend to man.
People always receive his friendly smile
And a feeble wave of his hand.

You may have wealth for people in need
And can lift a brother's load,
But the old, old man in his squeaky old chair
Gives a smile and a wave to the road.

Note:

My mother had a gift of seeing beauty and purpose in situations where other people saw nothing more than daily life. This poem is a great example of that.

Near the highway outside our town, stood an old house in need of repair. On the front porch sat an older gentleman—seemingly all the time—patiently watching for cars and passersby.

Once seen, he would always raise his arm and, with a gentle wave and a smile, greet each and every traveler.

In this she saw—and here she expresses—the power of a simple act of encouragement and giving to others whatever you have to give, if only a smile and a wave from beside the road of life.

I saw him routinely but likely would never have thought of him again, except for his legacy living in this poem. Now I think of him often and his action has influenced my life because of mom's gift.

– John C.

Where are the Bad Men Buried?

Where are the bad men "buried?"
The sexton was asked one day.
"I find no *evil* men buried here,
Were they just put away?"
The sexton shook his grey old head,
And with his kindly old voice he said,

"I have labored in this place,
For half a century of years.
I've heard the moans of broken hearts
And seen their bitter tears."

Then he lifted his careworn face and said,
"There are in this place no wicked dead.
For who can say when a loved one is gone
That he was a sinner and that he lived wrong.

It's better to see some good if you can,
Than to tell the world, here lies an evil man.
When men have been bad let it die with their bones;
We don't write it down on cold tombstones."

Meet Me There

Not leaving home; just going home.
Saying Goodnight here; Good Morning there.
Death is not the end; only the beginning.

The bugle calls no longer
    to arouse the servant to labor,
But the sound of the trumpet calls
    to freedom and rest.

Toiling ended, suffering over,
No more parting, pain or sorrows;
    the contest is over
And the award of peace is granted.
    The half has ne'er yet been told.
The house of the Lord is filled with glory.
    A white robe of purity, immaculate
And the great white throne
    Sanctity of heaven... meet me there!

–February 8, 1973

Life

Life, we have been together through pleasant and
through cloudy weather.
For a long time you have seen my mistakes,
yet you have given me courage and faith
to profit by them.

You have taught me to be happy amid even
the drudgeries.
How to live, love, hope and how to pray.
How to cope with things as they are,
Not as I would wish them to be.
To look at myself more and others less
When gazing in the mirror of souls.

Life, you taught me that there are pleasant valleys,
also steep hills.
But life, you have given me a loyal heart.
I hope I have measured up
to the demands you have made of me.

Life is a mission to be lived with a purpose.
Improve it and be happy—
despise it and be wretched.

Life is above profession, calling or creed.
Material wealth cannot add to its value
Poverty cannot take from its worth.
A full Christian life leads to heavens' gate.

Starting at birth it runs through all eternity.
When the light of heaven streams
through the mist of death.
May there be joy and peace.
My soul redeemed and purified.

April 14, 1974

Zona was the baby of the family, circa 1904

Her Home & Family

I Must Get Home Before it Grows Dark

My father made rules
And we children obeyed;
"Be home before dark"
Was one rule that he made.
The mile seemed so long
When school day was done.
But we always reached home
Before the setting of the sun.

Lord I must get home
For dark is the night.
Oh Father in Heaven
Please give us the light.

Zona's childhood home looked a lot like this. A lot.
No known pictures have survived of the actual residence.

My Old Home

I am thinking of a house of gold,
It wasn't bought, 'twas never sold,
But built by a loving Father's hands,
for years it stood storms' shifting sands.
It's humble roof and splintered floor,
rusty hinges on a friendly door
Which was never closed, it had no bar—
but its welcome sounded near and far.
An open breezeway and a hall,
that hinted room enough for all.
The old fireplace where fires burned bright
The crystal panes and the oil lamplight.
A big old house where children played.
And the pattern for Christian living was laid.
Youth swiftly passed on flying feet.
The years seemed long, but days were sweet.
Oh happy house of gold,
you're here no more and now I'm old.

Written in memory of my own home
nestled in the hills of my own Kentucky.

–Z

Reflections on Loss and Thanks

We are all so grateful for sweet sad memories
of Father, Mother, sister, brother.
We sigh for the touch of a vanished hand
and the sound of a voice that is still.
Yet we look forward to a fond reunion
in a "Land that is fairer than day."

Faith in God is the basis
of our hope for the future.
Faith is the comfort
in all our affliction.

I am grateful that God gave, and has given me;
my seven grandchildren
and my three sons
and daughters-in-law.

I am thankful for my companion;
for his nobility
his attentive kindness
his constant concern for my comfort
and my welfare.

I try to understand and appreciate him
and walk beside him
along this short journey of life.

I don't want to run before him
for he is the head of my house.
1 don't want to drag behind him
and become burdensome.
I want to stand with him
to help to comfort

To be a true companion.

January 20, 1974

Silent City

In the fairyland of childhood,
In the care free days of youth.
Carried to the silent city
Where so early I learned the truth.
Where I saw my mother weeping
And I heard my sister's cries,
I knew not their hearts were breaking,
They were saying sad good byes.
Too young was I to know the meaning,
Why I saw the upturned sod.
But my Grandpa's house looked lonely,
So strangely old and odd.
Later in life I learned the lesson
When in sorrow tears I shed.
When my mother too had gone
To the city of the dead.
O'er land and sea I wandered
But every place where I did roam,
At the edge of every city
I would find those white tombstones.
But thanks to God in heaven
There will be no upturned sod
When I move to that new city,
That beautiful city of God.

The Dream Path

Mother, you walk upon
the dream path of my sleep,
And in my waking hours
I feel the blessings of your smile.
Although the years have fallen
like autumn leaves,
You have walked beside me
mile by mile.
Some golden evening we shall meet again.

Reluctantly I will look back
on unfinished tasks.
Then you will take
my trembling hand in thine,
And say, "Tired child come on,
God guides the future as he has the past.
Heaven is a beautiful place—
Be thankful now, and realize,
Although you labored here to please the Lord,
In heaven for you he has a sweet surprise."

The Empty Pocketbook

I lived in the mountains
When I was a little girl.
Just a small place in the country
We little knew about the world.
But we went to church on Sunday,
We had no building bright and fair,
Just a little country school house—
Yet I learned that God was there.
When the preacher from the city
Came to bring the message sweet.
But no money had the people
His expenses to help meet.
I saw my daddy walk up humbly
Lay two dollars on the stand
And I saw the empty pocketbook
He hid in his other hand.
Mother said as we were leaving,
"There's no flour in our bin."
Then reproving, Daddy answered,
"Leave the miracle to Him,"
When the sun was low at evening
Daddy took me for a stroll,
On the ground in Daddy's vineyard
Something green lay in a roll.

Yes, the miracle had happened;
        Daddy's faith had made him wise,
For the little roll was money;
        Tears fell fast from Daddy's eyes.

Have faith—
        And leave the miracles to Jesus.

Logan Chapman tending one of his famous vineyards
Circa 1925

Toils Ended

I saw him in the days of youth.
He placed the seal of our love upon his heart;
Love as strong as death.
I lived in his shadow with delight.
His voice was sweet; in his strength I relied,
On his strong arm I rested.
His law was the law of kindness; his lips spoke truth.
With others he toiled, rejoiced and sorrowed.
But the shadows are falling and evening draws near,
His wavering steps falter.
I see him pause and sit by the wayside,
and his feet seem to stumble when he rises again;
He must have help—he has helped others.
For the days are now closed on his daily labors.
His working tools lay idle, they are rusting away.
Father as well as mother have looked well
to the welfare of the family.
He has never eaten the bread of idleness and
Thank God his children arise and call him blessed.
A man that feareth God,
He shall be blessed.

1972

Father Logan and Zona, circa 1927

From Zona's notebook: About this poem...

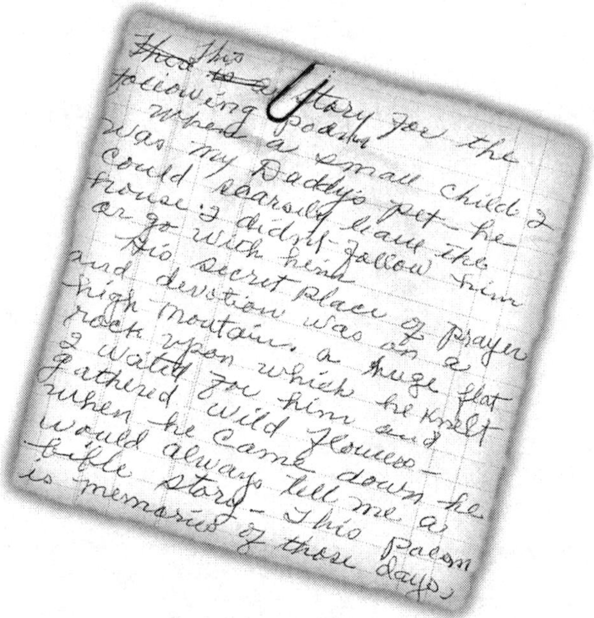

This following story for the poem
When a small child I was my Daddy's pet - he could scarcely leave the house I didn't follow him or go with him
His secret place of prayer and devotion was on a high moutain. a huge flat rock upon which he knelt I waited for him and gathered wild flowers - when he came down he would always tell me a bible story - This poem is memories of those days.

When a small child, I was my Daddy's pet—he could scarcely leave the house that I didn't follow him or go with him.

His secret place of prayer and devotion was on a high mountain—a huge flat rock upon which he knelt. I waited for him and gathered wild flowers. When he came down he would always tell me a Bible story.

This poem is memories of those days.

–Z

My Father's Altar

I must go back
to the forest deep,
where the isles are dark
and the mountains steep.
There's a sylvan call
from the mossy cleft,
where I must learn
from secrets kept.

I must kneel again
to nature's God
upon the mountain pansy sod
and drink again
from the crystal stream
and fill my soul
with God's love beams.

February 7, 1971

To My Daddy

You said you would come when lights were low
Even at midnight—
        your spirit I would know.
And I look at the glorious stars away up in the sky
We are always there together—
        your wonderful spirit and I.
I seem to see them clearer than in my youthful days,
They seem to draw me nearer—
        up to the great white way.
And when I walk in your garden
and look at your beautiful flowers—
        I know you are there with me.
And no communion is like ours; you said we were pals
That we would be pals in heaven together—
        pals through eternity.
We will walk in God's flower garden
So happily hand in hand—
        Just like we used to, Daddy,
When you sang of that beautiful land.

Logan Crittenden Chapman, circa 1935
1867–1937

Your life is a poem Daddy,
a poem delightfully read.
I read it over again
and to me you are not dead—
You beckon me to follow.
You ever hold my hand.
All will be joy and gladness
when we two meet again.

Daddy passed away 27th of June 1937

–Z

Mary Elizabeth Spencer Chapman, 1863–1949, circa 1935

NOTE:

Mom loved her mother with a marvelous level of honor and respect. It was always interesting to me, and a little out of place, that grandmother smoked a pipe—for eighty years. An older sister, Aunt Marg (hard g), smoked and she would give her four-year-old sibling the pipe full of tobacco and ask her to put an ember in it from the fireplace and puff on it to get it started. Grandmother developed the taste and habit and kept both until her death in 1949, at age 86.

– John C.

Mother's Yellow Roses

It was dusk and we walked together,
Yellow roses were in bloom,
She plucked and pressed one to her lips
Inhaling their perfume.

"Yellow roses are the sweetest,
Yes, they are my choice,"
All the while I silently listened
To my dear Mother's voice.

Now long years have come and past,
Years since she has traveled on,
But we walk together in memories
When yellow roses sing their song.

Golden roses now are blooming
In her garden up above,
The sweet dreams we wove together
Were rose buds of mother love.

Mother's Face

She was such a darling mother,
She's been gone for quite awhile,
Tear drops tremble on my lashes,
Memory of her brings a smile.
I, the youngest of her daughters,
Always with her. Now it seems
I can see her in the distance,
Smiling at me in my dreams.
She was such a tender mother.
We were pals for many years.
Happy, doing things together,
Memory brings to my heart cheer.
Thank God for a praying mother,
Oft I've heard her in the night.
Asking God to keep her children
And to lead them to the right.
I shall ne'er forget the moment
And the look on her sweet face
When she fell asleep in Jesus
Who'd prepared for her a place.

March 23, 1968

My Mom

The world don't seem quite the same, Mom,
As it did when you were here.
We miss the links in the chain, Mom,
Since Jesus called you up there.
We'll visit with you again, Mom,
When God is through with us, too.
But we have to linger here awhile, Mom,
Until he calls us to be with you.
But today we remember your goodness, Mom,
Today we long for your smile.
We would like to cuddle our heads on your breast
And rest just a little while.

Zona's mother, Mary Spencer Chapman, circa 1930

Mother's Birthday

Mother, you came in a dream last night,

Put your arms about me and held me so tight.

I called in my sleep, "Oh, Mother dear!"

Did you know I was suffering?

Is that why you are here?

God gave me so much when He gave me you;

So much of heaven—so gentle, so loving,

Unselfish and true.

Zona's mother,
Mary Elizabeth Spencer Chapman,
was born March 23, 1863.

Mother, in Vesper Hour

It's evening time, it's vesper hour.
The chimes ring sweet and low,
There is perfect beauty in the pale moonlight.
Precious memories flit in the afterglow.
Out of my thoughts and out of my sight
You steal through the night to me,
And I try to close my eyes and think;
You are real and so close to me.
But my heart cries out
Because you're not here.
And the moon beams grow wet with dew.
Then I kiss a message and blow to the stars
And wish I were up there with you.

1968

To Clara

I'd like to take you by the hand;
We'd wander back to fairyland
Where violets grew modest but tall.
Like the breath of youth it comes to me,
Where like the flowers we too were free;
Back home by the old waterfall.

The moonlight streaming through the trees,
The whisper of that southern breeze;
Those days we can't recall.
Many moons have come and gone,
Many friends have traveled on,
Since we played by the old waterfall.

But the trail won't take us back again;
Nothing but memories now remain.
My tears like rain drops fall
When I think of hours as sweet and gay
Where we played our precious youth away
Down by the old waterfall.

Someday I hope we meet again
In that beautiful land where there is no pain,
And unite with our loved ones all.
But tonight, I wish we could return
To the days for which my heart doth yearn,
The place of the old waterfall.

Daddy

Christian Daddy long departed,
Could I talk with you today?
I would tell you I have started
Following where you led the way.
When on your bed you lay dying
Then you gently took my hand,
"Baby darling stop your crying,
I am ready—understand?
I am going home to Jesus
Golden Streets and gates of pearl,
But I'm leaving you my baby
In a cold and wicked world.
You're a Christian, and I love you,
Always comforting your dad.
But you have three baby boys
Sweet as anyone ever had.
Hold their hands and lead them forward,
Teach them every day and hour.
They're your duty God has given;
He'll protect you with his power."
Daddy Darling I am happy
I have lived to see the day
That my boys are Christian soldiers
Walking in God's Holy way.

Who?

Who rocked me to sleep when but a small child
And comforted all of my fears with a smile,
And then labored so hard to give me a chance
To take my place among men?

Who wore old clothes that I might have new?
And thought there was nothing bad I would do.
Who banked on me to the end?
Who boasted of me when I was a youth?
And said, "There's a boy who always tells the truth?"
He made me his pal and his friend.

Who is growing old?
And the way growing dim?
Have I been a spiritual uplift to him?
Have I hurt his pride by neglect?
Have I let the light of his life grow dim?

What have I done for him?

50th Anniversary

I raise my glass to happiness,
To my Grandparents sweet.
These are the days of glad sunshine
Where all the family meet.
So here's a toast to happiness
As we never felt before,
They have been happy for fifty years,
And we wish them fifty more.

Written in 1967 for Cornelius and Minnie Estes—
the parents of Zona's daughter-in-law, Joyce.
It was read at the celebration by their
granddaughter, Janet Bass.

Wings

She does not know
What may await,
Or what the morrow brings,
She only knows
The time has come
When they must try their wings.

No longer will she walk with them,
To share their joy and pain,
But her battered heart
Repeats the thought
"Life will never he the same."

She taught them to be tall and true
And from apron strings be free.
But to make her heart be free from them?
That time can never be!

So, she gave them smiles
And cheered them on,
Wishing them happy days.
And when they were gone, cried bitter tears,
For that's a Mother's way.

Dedicated to daughter-in-law Joyce
wife of John C.

Just Been Visiting

It isn't a house, it's a home
That speaks of Christian living,
Where all the family to the Lord
Their very best are giving.
It's influence is eternal, this little home
Where hearts are knit in Godly love,
Where every book and picture
Points the way to heaven above.
It's a place, to think, to work, to give,
To love, to laugh to play.
It's a place to worship Christ the Lord
And a quiet place to pray.
You see a mother kind and true,
You hear sons and daughter sing.
Across its threshold a father
Walks with grace, God's word to bring.
There's dignity in a house—when it is a home.
I pray God's blessings linger there
And may no member ever roam.

Spring 1972, following a visit with
John C. and family in West Lafayette, Indiana

To Bobbie

On her hand she wears my diamond,
In her arms she holds my son.
She gives to me the joy of living,
Gives me the will to carry on.
There is a path that leads to heaven
And it's paved with her sweet love.
We have walked along together;
More happy years we're dreaming of.

January 15, 1970
Bobbie is Zona's daughter-in-law
wife of Buster

Bobbie & Buster
with daughter Diane
1956

Awaiting in Heaven

The clock upon the mantlepiece
Reminds me someday life will cease,
This little motor in my breast
Wear out and take eternal rest.
This care-worn house in which I live
Must back to God my spirit give.
Someday—I smile and whisper this—
I won't respond to your fond kiss.
Like an empty shell that lies alone
I'm here no more the pearl is gone.
Springtime will fade and summer come,
But a voice you loved will then be dumb.
The melancholy night winds drear
Remind you I'm no longer here.
But all is well, don't weep for me,
For with my God I'll ever be.
Awaiting in that heaven fair,
For the ones I loved to enter there.

Loved Ones

They are not gone
why weep?
When we wake they are
yet with us.
For those who live on
in loving hearts
are never dead.
They enter our dreams
when we are asleep.
Though heavens and earth pass away.
Love never dies.

Zona at 14 with her family in 1916

Her Lover

Lovers

The leaves fall and wither,
    The early night winds sigh,
The sea has its time to roar,
    The bird its hour to die.

The golden memories that make our days,
    We view each one apart;
The love revealed in my lover's eyes
    Is the treasure of my heart.

When the door of love was opened
    'twas a thrill I can't forget;
It was heaven—for awhile,
    The memory is heaven yet!

Floyd and Zona's honeymoon photo (notice the shotguns) at the family homestead in Miller's Creek, Kentucky in 1927. We really don't know if they were demonstrating their well-known sense of humor, or their actual hunting skills.

Could I Be Your Angel?

After I am gone
Could I be so near you
That you'd never be alone?
Would you want my presence
Ever by your side?
Would you need me, Darling
Still to be your guide?
When storms burst asunder
Would you feel me near?
Just to touch you once more
And wipe away a tear.
We have walked together
Along this road of life;
You've always been beside me
Since I became your wife,
And as we walked together
Through all our toilsome years
You have born the heavy burdens
And laughed away my fears.
I don't want to leave you
To face the world alone.
Could I be your angel
After I am gone?

Floyd & Zona visiting in West Lafayette IN, 1973

Zona & Floyd, Sr in Wagersville, 1938

To Dad

My brother lives across the track;
He has a mind to pity me.
He enjoys the praise of men;
his acts are plain for all to see.
I do not doubt his deeds are good;
he cheers the sick and prays so loud.
He carries bread and wine to them;
he strives to please the cheering crowd.
My left hand knows, but answers not
to what my other hand may do.
But both are busy all the time;
they know the things they do are true.
And from a heart that is sincere
to serve my Father up above,
I sound no trumpet for my acts
for they are simply deeds of love.

Dedicated to my husband, Floyd Samples

–Z

Dad Samples

He is not rich
        Neither is he proud.
But he stands tall
        in the busy crowd
Giving his family
        the best of his life.
Constantly planning
        in the daily strife.
Hard knocks a-plenty
        and hard to bear.
Courage it takes,
        but he has his share.
Never complaining
        when things go wrong,
Still trying to help
        his loved-ones along.
Not many compliments,
        neither too many thanks,
But he will sure be missed
        When he falls from the ranks.

1967

Floyd Byrd Samples, 1978

The Last Day of Summer

Now the day is over, the hour is growing late,
What a glorious beautiful sunset—1968.

Could I have my summertime again?
The summertime of life I mean.
I think I would get myself married
to a tall and handsome man,
I would walk by his side so proudly;
I would be in love with him.
My life would be meaningful and beautiful.
I would repeat the same vow to the same man;
I would value that promise as sacred,
And keep it pure and true every minute of my life.
Every time I heard his footsteps coming home
I would fall a little deeper in love with him.
I would raise his sons to be gentlemen
and Christian.
I would train them to be tall and straight
like their father.

I would praise him
for what he is.
He would be my strength
in weakness,
point me to God's way,
when I faltered.
He would lure me
back to life
when death
seemed certain.
His attention and
tenderness
would always renew the
feeble hold onto life.

Yes another summer has
ended—life is a swift race.
Dear God, keep your hands
on our shoulders
and your voice in our ears.
Now and forever.

Photo:
Zona and Floyd, circa 1935

Note:

When I was born, my mother almost died; she laid seriously ill for many days.

It was Dad that gave me cuddling and comfort in those first days, while also tending to the chores of his business—the only general store in town.

Mom wrote these lines in his praise.

– John C.

Dad's Lullaby

It was almost forty years ago;
The memory brings a sigh,
For the happy scenes of long ago
And a Daddy's lullaby.

The little mother very ill
Lay on a sick bed near,
While Daddy rocked the baby
In a creaky rocking chair.

Each night when work was over
And the chores had all been done,
He came into the bedroom
And held his baby son.

Those memories are so pretty,
They almost make me weep,
When Daddy sang sweet lullabies,
And baby went to sleep.

1973

Every Day

Ev'ry day's been a wedding day
For your heart's been strong and true.

Ev'ry day's been a pleasant day
And every morning new.
For we have walked together
In this old game of life.

So I can say from my heart today,
"I am glad I am your wife."

November 22, 1967
on their 40th Anniversary

Floyd & Zona in Dayton Ohio, 1978

Adventure

The birds have flown away;
    The flowers are dead and gone;
The clouds look cold and grey,
    around the setting sun.

These are the words of my Daddy,
    Just forty-three years ago tonight,
How well I recall the last hours
    of my single life.

Daddy prayed for heaven's
    protecting power on me in my new adventure.

"Will he care for you as I have;
    Will he all your burdens bear?
You seem so small and childlike;
    You need someone to care."

Yes, I have had a good adventure,
    A companion brave and true.
A husband kind and thoughtful,
    For Daddy, he loved me too.

November 22, 1970
on their 43rd Anniversary

A Trip on our 47th Anniversary

You have nothing to do Hubby, Darling,
Nothing to do you say?
Then let's take a trip on memory's ship,
To the land of yesterday.

Let's go back to the church in the wildwood,
Nestled close to the base of the hill.
And listen to the songs they were singing,
And the sermons by dear Brother Bill.

It was the church's annual meeting,
There were sermons of joy and grace,
That's where we first met, Hubby darling,
Remember that sweet hallowed place?

Love fell like sweet Immortal dew,
A romance begun in our hearts proved true.
The angels seemed our love to recognize
For they crowned our life with a paradise.

Happiness was there within our grasp,
When heart met heart in our hands' first clasp.
In that mystic realm where romance dwells,
Love affirms that all is well.

And hearts abide their time,
A messenger by cupid sent.
A joy that made our love sublime
And our hearts content.

November 22, 1974

Zona & Floyd at their Ravenna store in 1949
that they built from the ground up.

To Touch

To touch your hand
Relieves my heart of fear,
The fire burns brighter
When I know that you are near.
To touch your hand
And walk gently by your side
As we journey toward the sunset
Where we ever shall abide.
To touch your hand
And lean upon your manly breast
Where long years I've sheltered
Where my tired heart finds rest.
To touch your hand.
When the day of life shall pass away
And angels come to carry me
To lands of endless day.
Then *to touch your hand*
In that morning after the silent years.
To know we are together
In the land of no more tears.

Should I Be Called

Should I be called
And should I go quickly
As lightening flashing
Before the summer rain.
Weep not that you were not beside me,
For tender hands of the Great Physician
Will have lessened my pain,
"And we shall meet again."

June 30, 1970

Note:

While I was at the hospital waiting for word from the doctors who were treating Mom after her heart attack, a lightening bolt struck just outside with a thunderous crack, and a summer rain storm fractured the six-week draught that we had been experiencing in Cincinnati. As I was preparing to do her funeral, this verse of Mom's reached out to me singularly from among all her writings.

To this day it moves me that Mom went quickly during a summer rain.

– John C.

Evening Time for Hubby and I

It's evening time.

The shadows are long. Silently the sun is beginning
to set in the golden west.

Together we count the shining bright stars in God's firmament.
We are listening for the call.

Slowly walking the finishing miles of a long journey.
Ready to cross the silent river

Looking for the luminous footprints of the Master,
which only the blessed can see.

Hand in hand we have woven into harmony
all the discords of life.

Early in life we closed the door to things of the world that
were vain and sought peace with our heavenly Father,
following the narrow path that leads to Heaven's rest.

Thank you Father in Heaven, for our understanding, for being
able to count the golden stars, even in the darkness of
affliction and death. Amen.

June 22nd, 1977

The Empty House

I passed by the house
and I looked in the window;
The shades and the curtains were gone.
The pane in the window
like the pain in my heart
Showed how empty within and alone.
The silence brought tears
that I tried to restrain
But we must have sun as well as the rain.
I thought of flowers
That were given me one day,
I held them so tightly—they withered away.
A lesson I learned many years ago,
What we love we hold gently
And then watch it go.
The clinging soft touch
of a baby new born,
The rising sun in the early morn
The companionship of a little boy
A mystic pleasure, a heavenly joy.
So we close our eyes to reasons unknown,
Leave the empty house
and walk alone.

Note:

Mom and Dad moved a lot, but there were good reasons.

Until 1962, Dad made a living buying and selling real estate—especially grocery stores. He would often buy these little rural or small-town general stores in distress, make them successful, then sell them at a profit. He did that eight times, and twice he bought and sold farm land.

Dad had only one 'paying job' his whole life—with the Kentucky State Highway Department.

He always seemed to fare well, providing for his family however he could, and we would have been regarded as a middle-class family for most of my memory.

Something about the gypsy lifestyle must have been in the genes, because between Joyce and I and John Wayne and his wife Bobbi, we have moved a total of 59 times (and their house is up for sale as we complete this book).

– John C.

Traveling Around

1928–29	Grandpa Samples = two years Daddy and me
1930	Then the house on the hill; we were three
1930–35	Miller's Creek our next abode; sons total three.
1936–37	Our happy years on Beattyville Pike
1938–39	Back To Walter's, always in sight.
1939	A longer road to College Hill
	But resolute and strong our will
1939–43	Our next love nest was Wagersville.
1943–44	South Irvine then gave us a call
1944–45	In White Oak we were on the ball.
1945	North Irvine just a little while
1945–46	Broadway where we lived in style.
	STILL STRONG NEVER WEAK
1946–47	Our next hope was known as Cow Creek.
	Like an old song says, "My Dear Love"
1947	We lived awhile in Cedar Grove.
1947	Then to West Irvine we could see
1947–48	Riches great in Heidelberg Lee.
1948–49	Millers Creek then called again
1949–52	Ravenna followed loss or gain.
1952–54	Richmond Road our fate to meet
1954	Ravenna once more we did repeat.
1954–56	Millers Creek our old stand by
1956–62	West Irvine live, do or die.

(continued)

1962 Lexington a sweet refrain
a little red house on old Halls Lane.
1963 But promises made are often broken,
We had to buy on old Penmoken.
1964–72 Now it's back to Irvine again
Where we settled down devoid of brain.
We hoped to stay and stop our pace
Forever at the Peyton Place.
1973–77 Landed safe in Lexington again
Here we are on old Halls Lane.
1977 Dayton, Ohio First Day of May
1979 Less than two years later, Floyd passes away
1986 Cincinnati becomes Zona's home till her last day.

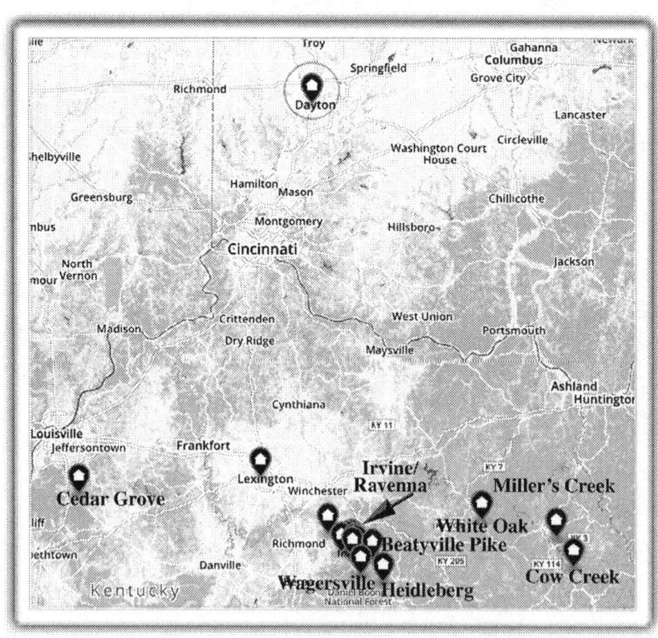

Zona's world—Millers Creek to Dayton

1957 and the beginning of a Thanksgiving family tradition.
The whole clan is here, except for Randy who would be
a later "surprise" for Buster and Bobbie.
Back to front: John C., Buster, Junior;
Joyce, Bobbie, Jean;
Zona, Floyd (holding Mereletta);
Roy (soon to be John) Wayne, Dain, Diane, Roxanna;
Billy (later to be Willie).

Her Three Sons

Three Beats of Love

I. In the darkness of the midnight
My newborn baby pressed
His little head against my heart,
And o' the loving tenderness!
Then I took an unknown journey
In a world of unknown pain.
Came so near the rippling waters—
But God brought me back again.

II. With quivering heart once more
I entered the valley of the shadow,
Anxious to bear the fruit of love,
Oh, precious mystery of motherhood
Lost in the depths of pain
Only to find another son,
And happiness when morning came.

III Then I heard a nightingale singing
On the night my last was born,
The sweet voice of the singer
Continued until the morn.
Although the night was anguish
I heard my sister pray
Then I heard the voice of my baby
At the breaking of the day.

Zona and her boys circa 1945
Back: Buster & Floyd (Junior)
Front: Zona and John

Those Little Ol' Boys of Mine

Sometimes in the silence of the vesper hour
When shadows creep from the west;
I think of sweet lullaby songs I sang
To my boys I lulled to rest.

Tiny boys with tousled heads
That long ago were mine,
I wonder how often they think of Mom,
Those little ol' boys of mine.

Now they are grown to man's estate,
So tall handsome and strong,
One could hardly believe
They were the wee lads
That slept by my lullaby song.

The years have altered my way of life,
But my heart is unchanged by time;
I am still the same mother
Who sang lullaby songs
To those little ol' boys of mine.

My Three Sons

Mother, when first you held your son
Did you then think of me?
When you ask me for one,
Behold I gave you three!

And in thy name, oh Lord
Thy grace I seek
Please Lord, may I find strength
To help the weak.

Along life's dangerous track
The journey's long.
Give me faith and wisdom
Don't let me fail to help the strong.

Touched by the virtue of thy spirit, Lord
Hold firm my hand.
And when I tread strange paths,
help them and me to understand.

And as I near the end
of things that be,
And I become a child myself,
May they help me.

Zona, Floyd, Jr., & Floyd Sr., 1929

An Angel Vision

I Saw her first look at her new born babe,
And her face lit up with joy.
'twas an angel dream just now come true
When they said, "he is a boy."

So she carved her dreams into his life,
For she had an angel vision.
She had no wealth but carved his soul
With the knife of love's incision.

The son grew and he is a man,
Heeding his mother's teaching.
A man among men,
Whom God has blessed,
And his influence is far reaching.

To Floyd Samples. Jr.
the first of her three sons

My Baby's Hand
(Three sons)

Some say the days are dreary,
        But it's not been so with me,
For in thoughts I travel backwards
        And play with my boys three.
We stroll through autumn woods,
        And through a valley wide.
We see so many pretty things;
        A hill, a stream, a mamma cow
        With her baby by her side.
The scolding voice of a blue jay,
        The song of the mocking bird,
The little one who walked with us
        Whose talk was yet unheard.
Though he jabbered along incessantly
        While the others ran with joy,
I understood the meaning
        Of the words from my baby boy,
As he looked at me so earnestly
        Trying to make me understand.
My heart races with joy
        With my three sons
        And the touch of my baby's hand.

Zona with boys and the family car, circa 1941
L-R Junior, Mom, John C., Buster

You Teased Me in a Dream

Why did you tease me darling? Why didn't you let me sleep?
I didn't want to punish you and then awake just to weep.
You were only four years baby,
        and you ran away to the stream.
I feared you would be drowned,
        and I had such a frightening dream

I called you but you laughed and teased me.
You caused me to stumble and fall.
Although I was wet and angry,
        you wouldn't come to me at all.
Until I broke a limb from a willow,
        then you ran to me with speed.

You put your arms around me, but my anger did not heed.
I stroked your legs; oh, baby forgive me.
It really wasn't wise and I felt so awful guilty
when I saw the big tears in your eyes.

I awoke from dreaming darling, then I was the one who cried
For you are forty, baby, and no longer walk by my side.
(I wish you were four and wading in the stream.)
Dreams are mysterious things.

I saw you so plain it was so real,
running up stream through the clear cool water.
I was after you angry and wet—
but you were my baby again.

Then I awoke, and it was only a dream.
Did it really happen that quickly
from four to forty?
Seems like it did.

Why do little boys have to grow up?
It would be a heavenly place on earth
if I could have kept mine like they were
when you were four.

I guess that's a silly thought, but a sweet one.
Yet, you have given my heart great joy in your sons,
and you have both shared them with us
for which I thank you, and I thank God.

They are the best—and so are you.

Sweet Dream

Last night I dreamed a sweet, sweet dream:
I was living in Millers Creek, it seems,
My kitchen was large and warm and wide,
And a little boy played by my side.

Through the mystic dream I could see,
Things just like they used to be.
Then he brought his little red wagon around
Said, "Mother, now let's go to town."

Down the road about two mile
I felt so tired pulling my child.
And Fayette Howell came along
Gave my arms a rest; my heart a song.

With the little boy in his arms
I felt secure, safe from harm.
There I saw his brown legs draggin'
Says, "Mother, where did you put my little red wagon?"

And where did I put my baby's red wagon?
Dream ended.

August 18, 1977

Empty Rooms

Just a wave and a kiss from my darlings
One more word and they are gone.
Still I hear their echoes saying
"Bye Mom, we'll be back soon."

But my heart aches, and it's lonely
Here in the twilight gloom,
Lord, please keep my heart from breaking
In these silent, empty rooms.

There was music, fun and laughter,
When they were here at play,
But I'm left with only memories
Of a happy yesterday.

I tried to keep from crying,
Lord you know I did my best,
But now my tears are falling
Like rain in an empty nest.

My heart aches and it's lonely
Here in the twilight gloom,
Please keep my heart from breaking Lord
In these silent empty rooms.

Fairy Land

The door opened and closed
and they were gone.
But in the brief time
they were with me
I dreamed of joy so sweet
That I pitied people in paradise.

I was so happy, my heart so glad,
Roaming and dreaming with my three lads
Walking along, holding their hands,
Skipping over mountains,
entering fairy lands.

We were a tribe of Indians
I was their squaw.
They were a band of bad men
I was the law.

Yes, summer is now ended,
I knew it couldn't last.
Since they are gone all that's left me,
is echoes of the past.

A little boy a fishing
  Another with a car
Sweet music comes a stealing
  He is playing his guitar.
Tenderly peal the bells
  of memory's chimes

Those were happy times.

Junior and John C., circa 1941

Baby

What do babies bring so rare?
Days of watching, hours of care.
But they make your day worth while.
Repay you with a baby smile;
Stammering tongue trying to talk;
Chubby fat learning to walk;
Rosebud fingers, grasping your hand;
Large wet kisses, oh! so grand!

Bind your heart with cords of love
To the heavenly Father up above.
Only a little baby,
A soul of God's design
A flower unfolding daily
So delicate and fine.

What are you dreaming of baby dear?
Smiling in your sleep?
Did angels open Heaven's gate
And permit you a little peep?

Your First Present on My Birthday

"An orchid, Mother to you!
And may it tell of my love—
A love and devotion that both combine
In wishing you happiness,
Mother mine."

My son gave me for my birthday this gift and no other
Just the picture of an orchid, to me his own dear mother.
Only the picture of an orchid, that is what he gave to me.
And I even gave him the money, to purchase it you see.
But I'll keep that little picture, for it's a treasured memory
For his thoughts were of his mother, and he was only three.

Never has he forgotten a birthday for thirty five precious years
but todays gift was the climax, for his present brought me tears.

Happy tears it brought me, a sermon; its subject "Joy"
A message from the mouth of God, presented by my boy.
Never a birthday has been missed since that eventful day.
Never too busy in his work, Never too anxious in his play
To wish his mother a happy birthday!

My Will

I will to you a legacy
of lessons learned at Mother's knee.
Oh, in my will are treasures rare,
a "book, a song, and always prayer,"
Solomon's wisdom, Jepthah's loss,
with Christ to help you bear your cross.

I will to you a battle field,
With little David's courage wield!
Look not for allies in the strife,
A Christian leads a pilgrim's life.

I will to you a world that waits
With pleading eyes and aching hearts,
The night is coming—hurry fast,
They have no God and it is dark.

It is the sunset hour of time,
When atomic blasts shake the skies.
The dark hours are wet and cold
One cannot sleep while Nineveh cries.

I will to you hills
my feet have never trod,
And sweet scented blossoms
That bloom only on the great fields of God.

A deeper knowledge of God,
Than to me has been revealed
The touch of God's omnipotence,
When God, through you, many souls are healed.

Three sons in Wagersville, 1939

Music

Everything that the sun shines on
Sing!
Music makes the world weep, laugh,
wonder and worship.
It tells stories of love and hate.

It is at the marriage altar,
and by the open graves.
It is the lovers' art,
It is the incense of prayer.
Listen! Hear it in the trees when soft winds blow,
Or the rippling of the waters.

The birds of the air it cheers,
comforts, refines and elevates.
It raises man from earth
and places him near God,
The great music master of the universe.

Man does not create it—
He discovers it, and uses it.

June 1974

Acceptance

In the darkness of midnight
God draws near
When hearts are heavy
With grief and care.
In the silence of pain
of tossing and sighing
When crushed by the gloom
cast by dreams that are dying.
Faith grows stronger
As the Holy Spirit we meet,
We accept our sorrow
and prayer is sweet.

Written June 1976, the week before Buster died

Buster playing and singing with his favorite Gibson
Date & Artist unknown

To Buster

In hours of happiness, I said,
"Take away my dream—its cold and dead."
My sweet spirit is soaring high,
I am content in my present sphere,
The web of my years are woven here
No need of a dream have I.
But I walked to the edge of the world it seems!
My heart cries out—give me back my dreams.
The years have made me wise
And as I walk with silent tread
If dreams are gone—the soul is dead;
In faith and dreams, I'll rise.

Zona's middle son, 'Buster,' a country music singer and producer, died at age 45 a few days after this writing in 1976 following a battle with cancer.

Buster and Zona at the Chapman homestead, circa 1950

June 7, 1976

The things of the world mean less—
my darling was carried away today.
He left this world of trials and worries
yet he seems nearer than before—
my love for him was a mother's love for her son.
It will never grow less,
but brighter will be that great unknown where he abides.
He is with God's son—
they will someday welcome me
to my new home in that happy land of bliss.
My spirit grows calm
and when the purple shadows fall
I will hear his voice singing
Amazing Grace, his favorite hymn.

Walter Roscoe (Buster) Samples
born February 17, 1931
Second of three sons.

Flowing on Without Him

The quietness of the evening as she sheds her parting smile and retires behind the curtain of the west, leaving the world to loneliness—and to me.

How can the year be already half gone?

The clouds gathered so quickly and bathed the first half in
 silent forbidden tears,
 fears and heartaches,
and it seemed one long night of tossing and turning without any restful sleep.

Now that it's over
 the agony,
 the looking forward to nothing,
 holding on,
 praying for God's wonderful grace to supply our hearts
and sustain us with comfort, for indeed it was a time of need.

Now oh, God , it was your will to take our loved one out of his suffering. His spirit remains, his influence will live on and on.
 He was tired, now he is at rest.

His tears are dried, the hidden tears that he never let fall, tears from an anxious heart for those who refused to do thy will.

He was tired
from burdens he bore for them,
for love's sake,
for Christ's sake.

So little of this world's honor his heart craved,
so much he deserved.
He loved people, and people loved him.
His influence was with people of all walks of life.
He was all that and more.

So for now the river of life flows on—
we leave our treasure with God,
making music on golden instruments,
smiling happy for ever more,
and all is well.

–Mother

July 10, 1976

My Second Son

Oh, Lord, we long for one
Gone home to be with Thee.
So weary, so restless of the night,
He watched the sun sink slowly
And smiled "because the scene was bright."
And bowed his precious head
Upon your loving breast
So sweetly at evening time
When the sun set in the West.
How happy he must be so close to you,
Please let me come to dwell with Thee
When my night falls too.

His last words were
Psalms 23

Buster went away June 7th, 1976

–Z

The Whispering Pines

Invite me to rest
And visit the graves
Of the ones loved best.

Grandparents and parents
And my child all gone,
My river of tears flow rapidly on.

Here I linger awhile
But I'll soon travel on
To that haven of rest

Where there's no tombstones.

June 1976
following Buster's passing

My Son

He came last night while I was sleeping
Caressed and petted me.
He was so strong and healthy
As beautiful as a man could be.
He smiled and said, "I love you,
In so many different ways."
And then just like it used to be
said, "what's for dinner today?"
Why did you come at Christmas time,
To comfort my poor lonely heart?
For awhile my world was heaven
And you were drawing me apart.
Apart from the crowd at Christmas
Who seemed so happy and gay.
You never failed in all my life
To make Christmas a happy day.
And you didn't this time
even though you
were with the angels.

Sunday, December 26, 1976

Remember Us?

Away, away, down in old Kentucky,
There's a little Mom and a Dad,
And you know they'd like to hear;
A letter would make them awful glad,
So sit down and write them (If you want to).

Sometime let them cross your mind,
They're not growing any younger.
Let them hear "just any old time."
Yes I know you're awful busy
At your age, we were busy too.
But the pleasure then was ours dear;
We were doing things for you.

Daddy now is quickly living up
His three score years and ten,
Mom is padding close beside him;
Time writes fast with her last pen.

So go ahead and write us (if you want to).
It would surely please our mind,
Just to look within the mail box
and there from you a letter find.

From Jerusalem to Emmaus

"Was not our hearts burning within us, while He spoke to us in the way, and He opened to us the Scriptures?"

It was Cleopas and his friend. However and wherever Christ talks with us and walks with us, doth not our hearts burn within us? Do we not call it inspiration? When it comes from the word of the "Master of Life."

The road to Emmaus was rough—part of it went through a narrow gorge, rocky and steep. We make our decisions, we suffer our defeats and failures. We travel to Emmaus but it's worth it all to sit at the Master's table and partake of the evening meal with Him. Being served by the hands that healed, hands that blessed, hands that raised up the dead, beautiful hands breaking bread and blessing it.

Oh, how great it is for you to give generous helpings to the hungry. 'Yes' to cowardly impetuous Peters, to loving Johns, to doubting Thomases, even to unfaithful dark hearted Judas—and say "take, eat!"

May I repeat General Douglas McArthur, which applies to you: "humility, for you have learned the simplicity of true greatness, the open mindedness of true wisdom, the meekness of true strength."

Even though many are around us—just a few words from you reveal a multitude of pleasures to my heart for I am always listening.

You are so much a part of my heart—my thoughts, my life—I need you. Forgive me but in my heart you are still "my baby" but in reality you are God's man.

To my son.

December 3, 1973

My Baby John

I heard the nightingale singing
On the night my child was born.
The sweet voice of the singer
Continued until the morn.
Although the night was anguish
I heard my sister pray
And then I heard my baby cry
at the breaking of the day.
If I could write as poets write
What to my soul is most delight
It wouldn't be the harvest moon,
Or the sweet scent of a rose in bloom,
The beauty of the star that glows,
Or mountain summits topped with snows,
The upturned earth with virgin sod,
Like a snow-white page from the book of God.
When He said, "I have finished,"
The earth and heaven, and man shall
rest one day in seven.
Nor would it be the beauty of morning,
With all its glories of God's adorning,
Then what to my heart could bring such joy?
Just the simple cry of my new born boy.

Written September 1, 1933
the same day 'Baby John' was born.

Messenger

I have seen him cry
When no tears were falling,
I have heard him sigh
Though his lips wore a smile.
I have seen him bend
With the day's heavy burdens.
Yet zealous for his Master,
He would walk that last mile.
Lured by the gleam
of a heavenly vision.
His labors are toilsome
Weary and long.
With thorn-torn hands
He has planted his roses
For the glory of God,
And he will still carry on.

For John C. Samples
by
Mother

The Minister Son

Go ye into all the world, and preach the Gospel to every creature. And lo I am with you always, even unto the end of the world. He, that goeth forth weeping bearing precious seed, shall doubtless come again with joy, bringing his sheaves with him.

The farmer often sows the seed and the drouth, or pests destroy. He gathers nothing for all his season's labor—but not so in sowing the seed of the Kingdom.

Minister, "be steadfast, unmovable, always abounding in the work of the Lord, For as much as ye know that your labor is not in vain in the Lord."

Sometimes a period of time must elapse before reaping can be experienced. But reaping is assured—we may not know the path the soul travels. But God gives the reward to the worthy. "They that turn many to righteousness shall shine as the stars forever and forever."

The minister suffers many heartaches; sometimes I am sure he feels like a curtain separates him from the people he is working with and for. Like walking into a crowd of men all laughing loudly, trading jokes, just having fun in easy going conversation. Yet there falls a hush, a quietness, the gay mood seems to vanish, they speak and act in a more courteous manner.

I am sure the minister doesn't want to be alienated, neither does he want to be placed on a pedestal—he is a man with personal problems, heartaches, financial troubles, and moods when he too likes to share the more human side of life with fellowmen.

Yes, Jesus walked the road to Emmaus; Jesus visited his friends; He was anxious about his Mother's welfare, (even in death). Yes, the minister is human and there is loneliness in the clergy life. He too has pains and hurts inside him—he needs friends to talk to. He goes from crisis to crisis, deaths, accidents, sickness, while giving comfort. They pour themselves out for others, but how many try to comfort him? They are scarce.

Jesus went about doing good for God was with him. Yes God is with you in winning souls to His glory. Love for lost souls—wonderful and happy is the man when his life reflects the light of God's divine love.

Love in the heart makes the burden light. A useful life motivated by love becomes effective—eloquence, skill tenderness and pity. It is a life without an end.

Minister, you are a great encouragement to your.... MOTHER

Her Grandchildren

Christmas With Our First Grandchild

Thanks for the invitation!
Your home was warm and sweet
With toys scattered on the floor
And the patter of our darling's feet.
Thanks for letting us share him.
Our house was cold and grey,
The winds swept up the valley
And time just wouldn't pass away.
There were no baby stockings
To hang up by the hearth,
There were no trills of laughter
To bring us peace on earth.
The peace the baby Jesus brought,
When in the manger he lay.
Thanks again dear children
For a happy Christmas day.

December 1951

Dain and Granny down on the farm with Brownie
circa 1953

Master Dain Samples

Dear Grandson:

Your letter made me very happy.

You have taken upon your sweet young shoulders the responsibility of being called a Christian. I feel assured you are very conscious of what it means. You will be different from the average boys—for not too many have the good Christian parentage that you have inherited. Although the decision to be a Christian is yours, your parents have taught you what it means, and I am assured even at your tender age you know you have taken a great step. I believe you will do your best to live up to the greatest title anyone can wear on their earth—a follower of Christ.

Christ Jesus came to this old world for the purpose of saving people who were lost because of sin. He walked as men on earth that we might know how to walk.

We can study His life and live like him; He said He would always help us, all we have to do to get His help is ask Him and trust Him. Bad people treated Him very badly. There will always be bad people who will treat His children badly but Jesus will help the ones who are on His side.

You are a good boy Dain, and I am thankful to God that you have taken Jesus as your guide and friend.

He is the light of the world.
He is the bread of life.
He is the living water.

Study His word and make a leader. God needs you in His work.

You can choose a vocation in life and still find lots of time to work for Him.

I am a very happy Granny.

February 6, 1961

Dain (1951–1993)
was Zona's first grandchild;
son of John C.

On Dain's High School Graduation

The old horse is making his final test in this last year of high school. Going to be felt on this stirring planet; going to strike this world with lasting force?

Then concentrate—more persons fail from a multiplicity of pursuits than from lack of resources. The future of your career and the happiness of your family depends on one moment—one word—decision.

The time is now.

As you pass from this year to another course of study. Your life is based on your own quality. Avail yourself of all its opportunities.

Start your building now. Make your foundation solid. You can become a treasure, precious, polished and priceless—or you can just fill an empty place that might as well have remained empty for all the benefit the world receives.

In life you may rank obscure and unknown or you may make the bright lights of publicity. Your future is in your own power to mold at will, you cannot value yourself too highly.

You have to make the decisions in your youth. They are not for old age to decide, for then limitation interferes. There are many pursuits that seem brilliant and alluring, but you know the story of the moth and the flame. You cannot expect to live tranquilly and at your ease, but be up and doing.

Many social events must pass by unheeded. Not isolation or complete absorption in your work, but keep the compass trained on the point of achievement.

Don't choose anything that would hinder your work as a Christian—for that my son is eternal. You are a precious grandson with unusual qualities; don't forget it. Remember now thy creator in the days of thy youth—Solomon's words of wisdom. In that still and secret place where one lives alone with God, my dear boy, is the making of life.

Whatsoever things are true—
truth unveils the face of God.
Whatsoever things are honorable—
reverence things of worth.
Whatsoever things are just—
to be weighed in God's balance and adjusted by his scales of justice.
Whatsoever things are pure—
pure as gold refined by fire,
lovely as musical chords in a Christian heart.

Think on things of good report. God will give sweet contentment of his dear spirit and in his presence is life.

Think on these things for it is the mind
that makes the heart rich.

Roxanna

There is melody in your laughter,
There is magic in your smile,
There is music in your pensive mood
That makes my life worthwhile.
Your touch is like an angel's
Your beauty like a queen,
May your wishes all come true,
You are the sweet of sweet sixteen.

January 5, 1968
Roxanna is Zona's 1st granddaughter
Junior's oldest child

Roxanna, Granny, and Mereletta, 1959
at Pa's West Irvine General Store

To Mereletta

I know that God will care for me
And keep me through, the night.
For he tucked my pretty flowers to bed,
And closed their petals tight.
Then he painted all the clouds
With silver, gold and blue.
Turned out the sun and lit the stars
And bathed the earth with dew.
And when I knelt to talk to God,
About my little cares,
I felt sweet comfort in my heart
And I know He too, is there.

Mereletta is Zona's granddaughter;
Buster's youngest girl

To Diane

The first day I saw you,
like a pink rose bud in the nurse's arms,
you looked at me and the thrill
pierced my soul.
It has been one continuous cord of love
To bind our hearts together
Through time and eternity.

Diane is Zona's granddaughter;
Buster's oldest girl

My Guest

'tis Autumn now.
The song birds have flown
        And left an empty nest.
In solitude I want the day
        When you will be my guest.
The summer is forever gone
        When from you I must part,
Your presence satisfied my thirst
        And the hunger of my heart.
So I shall borrow Aladdin's lamp
        And wish upon a star,
That God will keep you safely
        And happy where you are.

To Diane Gail, Sept. '75

Faith Realized

Yes, I gave him the car keys today
and thought of the game we used to play.
Mother may I take a baby step today?
"Yes, baby son, 'old tousled-head' you may."
Mother may I take two large steps today?
And out of our hands to school our baby stepped away.

But my heart stands still for the giant step he took today.
He took responsibility and drove out of sight,
Down the lone highway.
I never saw those boulders in that road before today,
Nor heard that crash, nor saw those bodies carried away.

But what did my son's mother say?
Then I heard her sweet voice humming as she did her chores away.
She was hiding all her fears from me, but hey,
I mustn't let her down this way.
There's work I must be doing, I haven't time to play.
So I go to my little study and there I pray.

Dear Lord I truly thank you for giving my sons to me
And the truly Christian boys they're trying so hard to be
I thank you for their mother who cared for them, and see.

It made me so confident when from home I had to be
Tired and homesick for them all,
Yet I could sleep peacefully.

And I know dear Lord the time will shortly come
When we can't all stay together in our little peaceful home.
Now I feel better Lord, My faith neither weak nor gone.
But you'll understand it, won't you Lord
If I wait up until my son comes home?

Written in 1971 on the occasion of her youngest son's youngest son, John Wayne, learning to drive.
– John C.

Teenager

Put on your best clothes,
and celebrate this day
for the family's little boy,
has gone and run away.

But Another took his place;
just as good, I'll wager,
For he is tall and handsome,
and he is a teenager!

Written on the occasion
of the 13th Birthday
of Zona's third grandson
John Wayne; son of John C.

John Wayne at the Miller's Creek homestead, Easter 1960
with his mother Joyce, brother Dain, and Zona
"Granny Samples" behind him

Message to Dain

Your star is the star of knowledge,
Yet wisdom must be your guide,
Many have gained great knowledge
And for lack of wisdom died.

You have remembered now your creator
In the days while your heart is young,
While evil days are not upon you
And life is a glory song.

The invisible urge within you
To seek His mysteries dim,
Are the gifts of the great creator
They're the seed and issues of Him.

–Granny

February 6, 1961

Note: When I first read this I marveled at how well she captured my brother's thirst for knowledge, and even his adult struggles as he searched for truth. I was stunned when I realized she wrote this when he was only nine years old.

— JW

To John Wayne Samples

I hear a rumor going round,
That your long hair is touching ground,
And that it is difficult as can be,
For you to raise your eyes and see.
For me I guess it's only fair,
To pledge allegiance to your hair,
And all the privilege is your'n,
Whether you are shaved or shorn.
But think how awful it would be,
If in a grave emergency,
You caught your hair in a revolving door,
And revolved there for evermore!
Let's don't get worried, never fear,
We'll just discredit what we hear.
To wear long hair is no disgrace,
Sometimes it hides a GHASTLY face!

Fall of 1972

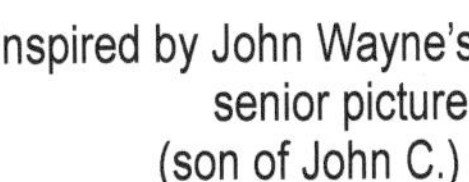
Inspired by John Wayne's
senior picture
(son of John C.)

...and then some

POEMS BY "ME"............JOHN WAYNE SAMPLES

My 'Granny' began encouraging me to write when I was just seven or eight years old. These clips from a Jr. High English class project are taken from a single page, typed and sent to her in 1967. Despite the typos—and just bad writing—she continued her encouragement until the day she died. Oh, and Dad NEVER said those things I said he said.

– John Wayne

DAD
HAPPY BIRTHDAY DAD,
BUT TO SAY IT IS SAD
THAT LITTLE OLE' YOU
IS A HUNDRED AND TWO.

MOM
MY MOM'S BIRTHDAY IS HERE,
IT COMES JUST ONCE A YEAR,
SHE'S HAD THEM SO OFTEN
SHE SHOULD BE IN A COFFIN
BUT LUCKY OLD MOM IS STILL HERE

DAIN
MY BROTHERS' BIRTHDAY IS HERE
I HERE NOT ONE SINGLE CHEER,
HIS NAME IS DAIN
AND I GET A PAIN
ABOUT THIS TIME EVERY YEAR.

ME
ME'S BIRTHDAY IS HERE AT LAST
YOU KNOW WHAT WILL SOON HAVE A CAST!
FOR THEY HIT SO HARD
I GO FROM HOUSE TO YARD
EVER, EVER SO FAST.

I LIKE MY PARENTS BUT I'M SURE I'D LIKE THEM MORE,
IF FOR MY BIRTHDAY THEY WOULD NOT GIVE ME SOMETHING
THAT WOULD MAKE ME SORE,
FOR LAST TIME, MY PANTS WERE TORE.
jws

OVER AND OVER MY DAD HAS SAID,
HE WISHED MY BROTHER, MY CAT, AND I WERE DEAD,
I DON'T THINK HE LIKES US VERY MUCH.
jws

jws

SHARP, BLACK TREES ON A SUNSET SKY,
MAKES ME PUKE!
SO I STAY AWAY FROM ANY TIES
THAT HAS SHARP BLACK TREES ON A SUNSET SKY.
jws

John Wayne Keep
this – It's real –
a treasure –
Granny
Sample

THE DAY STAR OF KNOWLEDGE OPENED UP TO ME
I FOUND IN ITS FIRST LUSTER, A CALL TO DESTINY
BUT IN THE FLUSH OF LEARNING OF THE TASK, THE CALL, AND THE NEED
I FOUND THE URGE TO WORK TOO GREAT TO IGNORE: I MUST HEED

THE URGE TO LEARN WAS WEAK INDEED, AND SEEMED VEILED IN SLOTH
THE WORLD WAS DYING, AND SOULS WERE CRYING: WHAT WAS MY EFFORT WORTH?
AND NOW THE WORK IS HERE AND HOW DOES MY FEEBLE WILL EMPLOY?
"MORE STUDY I NEED" AND THUS POTENTIAL FINDS FOOLISH DEPLOY.

JCS

Note:

A lot of the routine correspondence between Mom and I would include a verse or two about whatever was on our mind that day.

This is from a time in 1967 when I was trying to finish my undergraduate studies at Milligan College, and I was more motivated to write poetry than to write term papers.

– John C.

Note:

Granny's first grandchild was my brother, Alan Dain Samples. He was also the first of her grandchildren to pass away; she had been gone some five years when Dain died unexpectedly in 1993.

At the risk of being melodramatic...
My first reaction to dealing with my personal grief was an obsession to write. Looking back on it now, it was almost as if Granny was taking one more shot at putting her thoughts to paper, but instead of using her 'Poetry Ledger,' she was contributing through my computer keyboard.

It's because of that sense of her participation that I include a previously published ode to my brother beginning on the next page; her influence certainly was involved in the inclination to write, and maybe she even touched the words.

– John Wayne

Shadow On The Stage

The music has stopped, the curtain is drawn,
the last line is now delivered.
The words of the play, the soul of his song,
continue to be considered.
The Actor was good, he pulled us all in,
his success is easy to gauge.
Is he still there? Be still and listen,
for the shadow up on the stage.

I tried to do it, to be just like him,
this Actor I so admired.
He helped me along, through bright lights and dim
and always kept me inspired.
The roles got tougher, we were not lacking,
we both were now earning our wage.
He was an actor, I was just acting,
like the shadow, now on the stage.

To share with others, he turned to teaching,
to helping those who sought him out.
To learn for himself, he turned to reaching,
and seeking to answer his doubts.
I watched from afar, this tutor of mine;
he learned every word on his page.

We walked far apart, but always in rhyme,
that shadow, and me, on the stage.

The scene is not through, his role not complete
when the Producer calls his name.
The patrons scream "Foul," for none can compete;
the play, it just won't be the same.
His first student knows, though tries not to say,
the questions, the pain and the rage.
The Actor left this, when he went away:
left me, his shadow, on the stage.

What will we do now? The Actor is gone.
Will someone move into his place?
Can someone be found, to go it alone?
Will one fight his fight, run his race?
The answer is "No," for it will take two:
Those students the youngest in age.
His first pupil smiles, now slightly off cue,
at three shadows left on the stage.

John Wayne Samples
April, 1993

Dain, Granny & John Wayne, 1987

Her Endings

My Picture

There is in every heart a love for the beautiful;
Oh! artist paint what you see in me.
Do you see the spiritual elements of joy, peace and love?
And do you see sacrifice for right,
    pity for suffering,
    hatred for sin, and
    devotion to truth?
Will my picture be a masterpiece of beauty?
Are you painting what the eyes of others cannot see?
    What the camera cannot give?

Oh, Artist of the universe make me beautiful;
    paint the kingdom of heaven within.
May you see the surrender of my strength
    to always say "God's will, not mine be done."
Give me healing,
    sympathy to hearts in pain, and
    courage that knows not the loneliness of fear.
    A child-like faith with my hand in Thine.
To go thy way and to find a spiritual spring
    Where others say "mirage."
To know there is more joy in loving
    than there is in being loved.

Make me humble that you oh, Artist,
may see beauty through the dust of strife.
Teach me that tomorrow will its burdens bear.
Anchor my thoughts to the infinite in prayer,
that I may daily gaze upon the sapphire throne
and through Calvary's tears may I see Christ.

Do you see tolerance or smugness?
Help me to see how cold a visage righteousness
may wear, and hold a lantern for my stumbling feet.

Oh, great artist
of the universe,
make me beautiful
that my image may
be placed, not upon
the walls of earthly
fame, but within the
hearts of lives
whom my influence
has touched.

Zona's last portrait, 1988

John C. and Zona Samples, 1986

It is Finished

The most beautiful picture that I ever visualized
Has never been painted on canvas.
It is not a beautiful sunset,
Neither the dawn of the day
nor the scenes of my happy childhood
nor my precious children at play.
It isn't the face of my mother
though I loved her deep in my heart.
It's not the joyful look on my father's face
when he thanked me for doing my part
of the little tasks of a little girl
he'd assigned for me to do;
His grateful look made me happy
and I thrilled to his words, "thank you."
The most beautiful picture was painted in words,
by the beloved apostle St. John
And it gives me the most glorious feeling,
Of anything I ever looked upon.
It's the glorified picture of Jesus
When he talked to the Father in Heaven.
He said, "O' Father I have finished
All the tasks that to me you have given."
This picture cannot be painted,
Neither carved on wood nor stone.
The light in the eyes of my Savior
Can shine in men's hearts alone.

IT IS FINISHED

The old Covenant was nailed to the Cross (Col. 2:l4) and the New superseded it. All should be able to see and appreciate the superiority of the New Covenant (the Gospel) over the old (the law) and thank God that we are not under the yoke "which neither our fathers nor we are able to bear."

—Acts 15:10

The End

Z